# Bad Boy Bubby

# ✖ Controversies

Series editors: Stevie Simkin and Julian Petley

*Controversies* is a series comprising individual studies of controversial films from the late 1960s to the present day, encompassing classic, contemporary Hollywood, cult and world cinema. Each volume provides an in-depth study analysing the various stages of each film's production, distribution, classification and reception, assessing both its impact at the time of its release and its subsequent legacy.

**Also published**

Jude Davies, *Falling Down*
Shaun Kimber, *Henry: Portrait of a Serial Killer*
Neal King, *The Passion of the Christ*
Peter Krämer, *A Clockwork Orange*
Gabrielle Murray, *Bad Boy Bubby*
Stevie Simkin, *Straw Dogs*

**Forthcoming**

Julian Petley, *Crash*
Lucy Burke, *The Idiots*
Tim Palmer, *Irreversible*

'The *Controversies* series is a valuable contribution to the ongoing debate about what limits – if any – should be placed on cinema when it comes to the depiction and discussion of extreme subject matter. Sober, balanced and insightful where much debate on these matters has been hysterical, one-sided and unhelpful, these books should help us get a perspective on some of the thorniest films in the history of cinema.'
*Kim Newman, novelist, critic and broadcaster*

# Bad Boy Bubby

Gabrielle Murray

BLOOMSBURY ACADEMIC
LONDON • NEW YORK • OXFORD • NEW DELHI • SYDNEY

BLOOMSBURY ACADEMIC
Bloomsbury Publishing Plc
50 Bedford Square, London, WC1B 3DP, UK
1385 Broadway, New York, NY 10018, USA
29 Earlsfort Terrace, Dublin 2, Ireland

BLOOMSBURY, BLOOMSBURY ACADEMIC and the Diana logo
are trademarks of Bloomsbury Publishing Plc

First published 2013 by PALGRAVE MACMILAN

Reprinted by Bloomsbury Academic

Copyright © Gabrielle Murray 2013

Gabrielle Murray has asserted her right under the Copyright,
Designs and Patents Act, 1988, to be identified as the author of this work.

All rights reserved. No part of this publication may be reproduced or
transmitted in any form or by any means, electronic or mechanical,
including photocopying, recording, or any information storage or retrieval
system, without prior permission in writing from the publishers.

Bloomsbury Publishing Plc does not have any control over, or responsibility for,
any third-party websites referred to or in this book. All internet addresses given
in this book were correct at the time of going to press. The author and publisher
regret any inconvenience caused if addresses have changed or sites have
ceased to exist, but can accept no responsibility for any such changes.

A catalogue record for this book is available from the British Library.

A catalog record for this book is available from the Library of Congress.

ISBN: PB: 978-0-2302-9676-3
ePDF: 978-1-1373-6307-7
ePub: 978-1-3503-0649-3

To find out more about our authors and books visit
www.bloomsbury.com and sign up for our newsletters.

# Contents

Acknowledgements .......................... vii

Introduction ................................ ix

Synopsis .................................. xv

## Part 1: Somewhere between exploitation and art cinema

A Brief History .............................. 3
Casting .................................. 11
The Shoot: Cinematic Experimentation .......... 12
Festival Fame and the OCIC Award. ............ 17

## Part 2: Censorship, film festival classifications and pressure groups

Classification Exemptions .................... 27
Distribution, Neglect and Controversy .......... 35
The Italian Contradiction ..................... 38

## Part 3: Animal cruelty and the cinema

Animal Cruelty and Audience Affect. ........... 46
Laws and Regulations ....................... 49
The Peculiar Case of 'Crush Videos' ........... 55

Australia and Animal Rights. . . . . . . . . . . . . . . . . . . . 56
Domestic, Feral or Stray? . . . . . . . . . . . . . . . . . . . . . 59

## Part 4: Key scene analysis

*Huit Clos* . . . . . . . . . . . . . . . . . . . . . . . . . . . . . . . . . . . 65
Cockroaches . . . . . . . . . . . . . . . . . . . . . . . . . . . . . . . 68
Incest and Fear . . . . . . . . . . . . . . . . . . . . . . . . . . . . . 70
It's All about the Cat. . . . . . . . . . . . . . . . . . . . . . . . . . 73

## Part 5: Key themes

Media Outrage and Criminal Associations. . . . . . . . . 86
Sons and Mothers . . . . . . . . . . . . . . . . . . . . . . . . . . . 90
Disability . . . . . . . . . . . . . . . . . . . . . . . . . . . . . . . . . . 92
Innocence . . . . . . . . . . . . . . . . . . . . . . . . . . . . . . . . . 97

## Part 6: Legacy

## Appendices

Appendix A: Key Details . . . . . . . . . . . . . . . . . . . . . 109
Appendix B: Notes. . . . . . . . . . . . . . . . . . . . . . . . . . 112
Appendix C: References . . . . . . . . . . . . . . . . . . . . . 113

Index  . . . . . . . . . . . . . . . . . . . . . . . . . . . . . . . . . . . 125

# Acknowledgements

There are many people I would like to thank for their support and for their help in the preparation of this manuscript. Thank you to Rob Conkie for suggesting me as the author of this study. I am grateful to my editor Stevie Simkin for his patience and his insightful feedback, which greatly added to the clarity of the work. Ross Schnioffsky, research librarian at La Trobe University, made insightful contributions in the early stages of the work. Thank you to my postgraduate students Rajdeep Roy, for his technical advice, and Jade Jonteff, for her diligence as a research assistant. I am also thankful for the support of my colleagues in Media: screen + sound at La Trobe University.

As always, I am entirely indebted to my family 'the Murrays' and most importantly to Robert Beullens, who acted as both sounding board and reader, and who makes every day richer and sweeter.

All screen captures are taken from *Bad Boy Bubby*, 2 Disc (Collector's Edition), Umbrella Entertainment, Australia, July 2005.

# ✕ Introduction

Both parable and nihilistic comedy, *Bad Boy Bubby* (1993) focuses intimately on Bubby (Nicholas Hope), a distant, twisted relative of Werner Herzog's Kaspar Hauser. Bubby is a thirty-five-year-old man-child[1] whose *genitrice* keeps him imprisoned in a claustrophobic, windowless hovel. Terrifying him with tales of divine retribution and a toxic world whose polluted air will instantly kill him, Bubby's 'mother/keeper' Florence (Claire Benito) ensures his submission to her physical and mental abuse. In a perfunctory way, she feeds him, shaves him and washes him, and then at night she mounts him for her own sexual pleasure. Physically a man, yet emotionally a child, Bubby is hopelessly dependent on his captor/abuser to the point where incest is normalized and it becomes one of his only pleasures. His world is torn apart when his father, a charlatan and a sleaze, appears, usurping Bubby as his mother's lover. In this twisted, 'philosophical Candide style fable' (Rouyer and Ciment, 1995, p. 4), Bubby murders his drunken parents, suffocating them with cling wrap, and then escapes into what for him is the unknown 'real' world.

From the moment the Australian director Rolf de Heer's fourth feature, *Bad Boy Bubby*, took flight on the festival circuit in 1993, to its re-release in various DVD forms beginning in 2005, the film has polarized audiences. My brief description of its content is enough to suggest the film's uniqueness, but also its confrontational nature. While this volume will endeavour to examine how and why (on the festival circuit and during its first release) *Bad Boy Bubby* produced such conflicting responses from audiences, critics and classification and review boards, it will also assess its status nearly two decades on. What we can confidently say about *Bad Boy Bubby* is that it is still a film that ignites powerful and diverse responses. In the last decade, the various ways in which the film has been discussed include: a theological inquiry as to its stake in the idea of redemption (Stephens, 2011); a critical analysis of its experimentation with the use of multiple cinematographers and binaural recording (Cat Hope, 2004; Hicky-Moody and Iocco, 2004); as an exploration of representations of mental and physical disability (Ellis, 2008); and as a subject of grassroots activism with the film listed by online animal-rights communities and individual bloggers as one to boycott. As I will discuss later in the section on animal cruelty and the cinema, *Bad Boy Bubby* is high on the 'hit list' of many humane-society websites as a film to avoid due to its treatment of animals, specifically cats.

Censored by some and reviled by others, *Bad Boy Bubby* won numerous festival awards, including the prestigious Jury Prize at the 1993 Venice Film Festival. Today its impact on audiences seems to be just as strong; yet its legacy is difficult to assess. It is a film with a reputation that everyone has an opinion on; it's a 'one of kind' – both a winner of a religious award and a film that was boycotted due to claims that a 'cat was tortured to death on screen' (de Heer, 2010b). What is surprising, however, is that, despite all the hoopla, there is a paucity of sustained research on the film. De Heer has made a significant contribution to screen culture with the production of documentaries, television programmes and feature films. His thirteenth feature, *The King Is Dead*, had its Australian release in Melbourne on 12 July 2012. When it comes to discussing his work, de Heer is generous with his time and has given many interviews; however, D. Bruno Starrs's 2009 published thesis, *Dutch Tilt, Aussie Auteur: The Films of Rolf de Heer* is currently the only monograph that deals exclusively with his work.[2] It will be interesting to see whether de Heer's growing reputation, augmented in the last decade by his local and international success with *The Tracker* (2002) and the indigenous co-direction and production *Ten Canoes* (2006), will lead to a re-evaluation of his earlier work.

During *Bad Boy Bubby*'s original circulation, it attracted intense media attention, evident in newspapers, festival reports and film journals, but much of this writing is limited to short reviews and reports. The film continues to have a life in blogs and film-discussion hubs, cited either for animal cruelty or embellished with 'an air of mystique' (Finlan, 2005). It is labelled a cult object, one of those outrageous and bizarre films you must see and survive – yet, for all the controversy, little effort has been made to analyse it in detail. What discussion that has taken place around the film is generally of an odd kind; *Bad Boy Bubby* is perceived as an emblem of extraordinary humanity for some, yet for others it is bizarre, shocking – a sick joke. From both sides of this divide, the film is approached as a kind of banner or label, but something also to be shied away from, as though its content is unmanageable, unintelligible, perhaps even dangerous or contagious. Here I would like to offer my own anecdote as an example. Several years back I was asked to contribute a chapter to a collection on Australian and New Zealand cinema. This was my opportunity to write on *Bad Boy Bubby*, a film that I have always considered a flawed but singular phenomenon – brutal and heart-wrenching, with hilarious moments, at times a little heavy-handed, yet utterly compelling. My proposal was promptly rejected and I was asked to choose another film as a subject. The editors never gave me a clear answer as to why they opposed my choice, but nor was I completely surprised by the rejection. The unease around this film suggests that it is perhaps too strange, too controversial; certainly not a film to be valorized within the category of Australian national cinema, an already troubled discourse in the post-Mabo era (Collins and Davis, 2004),[3] and further complicated by the pressures of globalization.

In an attempt to rectify this situation, and in line with the *Controversies* series, this volume will focus singularly on *Bad Boy Bubby* and its critical status as a controversial film. Part 1 will place the film in the context of de Heer's work and the constraints of low-budget film-making. The casting and experimental nature of the film will be explored, and the section will conclude with a discussion of the film's award-winning success at the Venice Film Festival in 1993. Part 2 will examine the classification regulations around film festival screenings and distribution, focusing particularly on the controversy that arose in Venice at the time of its release, with claims that a cat had been killed on screen during the making of the film. A range of censorship issues will be discussed, including the disparity between the film's release in Australia, in the United Kingdom and in the United States. The film's notoriety, which was mainly generated by issues to do with animal cruelty, will be central to Part 3. The Acts and the regulatory bodies that have influenced the treatment of animals, specifically those used in media, will be addressed. The effect that the UK Cinematograph Films (Animals) Act 1937 and Animal Welfare Act 2006 have had on the treatment of animals in media will be examined, along with the influence of humane societies and the RSPCA. One of my main aims is to illuminate the ways in which the film produced conflicting responses through the close analysis, undertaken in Part 4, of the open sequence, the *huit clos* of Bubby's life, where the abusive 'mother-and-child' relation is established, and Bubby is seen to torment and suffocate the family's cat and murder his mother and father. Part 5 will outline thematic concerns explored in debates about abuse, incest, disability and mother-and-son relationships. Finally, Part 6 will discuss *Bad Boy Bubby*'s legacy, specifically in relation to how the singularity of the film's vision has resulted in its continuing relevance.

Interestingly, in his article on Australian film studies' contemporary obsession with 'ozploitation', Adrian Martin asks, 'Where did Rolf de Heer's *Bad Boy Bubby* ... go – surely as pristine an example of confrontational aesthetics and transgressive content within a straightforward narrative as one could wish for?' (2010, p. 15). The fact that the film has attracted little scholarly attention does have something to do with its strangeness, its uniqueness. For example, where and how do we place this film in the context of film history, of Australian film history? What mix of genres would best represent the film's content and style? François Truffaut's *The Wild Child* (*L'Enfant sauvage*, 1970) and Werner Herzog's *The Enigma of Kaspar Hauser* (*Jeder für sich und Gott gegen alle*, 1974)[4] are often cited as similar 'feral-children stories', while *Being There* (1979) and *Forrest Gump* (1994) are included as more commercial, sanitised versions. These films address the notion of 'the Innocent: the child-like individual who, by experiencing the mature world all of a sudden, is able to see through the corruption that everybody else has learned to take for granted' (Barber, 1995, p. 13). While, broadly speaking, *Bad Boy Bubby* does explore this theme, it is still difficult to identify a clear cinematic legacy. The film's low budget and gothic images of depravity mean that some critics feel comfortable placing it in the category of cult or exploitation, whereas the prestigious international awards and level of critical acclaim it has garnered would suggest that a more appropriate label could be that of art cinema with, as Tom O'Regan notes, an Eastern European sensibility (1996, p. 156).

The lack of extensive critique, however, is perhaps best understood through a discussion of the many ways in which this film offends audiences. For most of us, watching *Bad Boy Bubby* will, at one moment or another, induce feelings of enormous discomfort. In his original review of the film, David Stratton rightly noted that there was something 'to offend just about everyone. Among those likely to be outraged are the devoutly religious, feminists, animal lovers and the Salvation Army' (1993).

This monstrous story of a little 'Aussie battler' is blatantly 'politically incorrect', yet it is also challenging and redemptive. I would argue that the most probable explanation for its neglect is that it crosses too many boundaries – and breaks at least one too many taboos.

The film deals explicitly with physical, mental and sexual exploitation. Florence (or Mom), Bubby's mother, sexually and physically abuses him; blasphemy is rife; 'feminists' beat this *idiot savant*; and a policeman (Dave Flannagan) places him in a confinement cell, offering him as prey to a fellow inmate, 'the Animal' (Michael Constantinou) (2010a), who promptly sodomises Bubby. Out of all of these possibly objectionable events, the act generating the greatest controversy concerned Bubby's treatment of a cat. While discussions of censorship generally relate to perceptions of the potential harm to an audience, animal cruelty is a legal issue pertaining to any harm caused to an animal during the making of a film. Surveying the different responses the film received from audiences and classification and review boards in Australia and the US and comparing these to the reasons for its censorship in the UK will enable a better understanding of the relations between animal-rights laws, film censorship and social sentiments to do with the treatment of animals.

# ✕ Synopsis

Denying us any clear exposition, *Bad Boy Bubby* immerses us in a bunker-like room that has been Bubby's home and prison for the thirty-five years of his life. The film opens on a scene of a dowdy, grey-haired woman shaving Bubby; she then washes him as he stands in an old tin tub and prepares him a Depression-era meal of torn pieces of white bread, sprinkled with sugar and soaked in warm milk. For the first third (or act) of this film, we do not leave the stained-walled, starkly furnished, grimy interior of this bleak space. The woman (Mom) is Bubby's mother, captor and lover. She occasionally ventures out, face encased in a gas mask, leaving Bubby behind, having warned him to sit still. Having terrified him into believing that the outside world is poisonous and that an omniscient god watches his every move, Bubby complies with her demands. He sits still for hours, eyeing a headless crucifix impaled on the wall above him. When he wets himself or misbehaves she beats him, when he asks about the outside world she claims it is dangerously toxic, demonstrating its effect by covering his mouth and nose with her hands (see Figure 1), until he nearly suffocates. His only real comfort is the pleasure he receives from her cooing praise that he is a 'good boy' as at night she allows him to fondle her ample breasts, while taking her sexual fulfilment astride him in the bed they share.

Apart from his mother, Bubby shares his 'home' with cockroaches and a cat. Deprived of human relations, affection and other forms of communication, he spends his time copying the actions of the cat and the scuttling pests. His 'baby' speech is formed through mimicry of his mother's commands, praise and curses, occasionally interspersed with the sounds made by the unhappy cat. Dressing as his mother, he enacts her wrath, in curses, entrapment and abuse of the animal. One day, his world is drastically changed

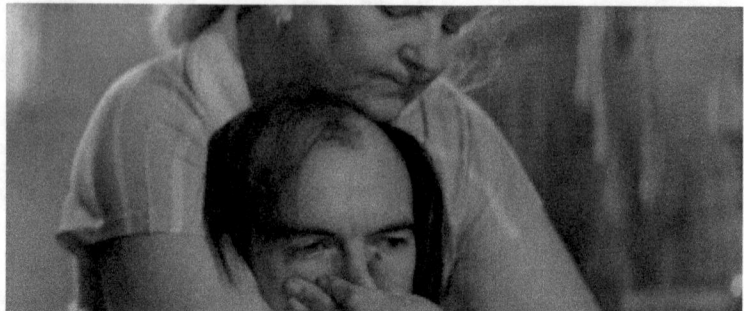

Figure 1: Mom demonstrates to Bubby what it feels like to suffocate.

when Pop (Ralph Cotterill), his unknown father appears. Pop is stunned to learn he has a son, albeit 'a weird one'. Bubby, usurped by his father as his mother's lover and regularly abused and beaten, kills both his parents when they return one night, drunk after an expedition into the outside world. Using the only tool he has available to him, he suffocates them with cling wrap, just as he had previously suffocated his cat.

Once realising the air outside will not kill him, Bubby packs his cling wrap-entombed cat into a suitcase and ventures into the world, for him a place in which everything is new and full of wonder (see Figure 2). The film then takes on an episodic structure, following Bubby as he stumbles through a range of encounters and exchanges that invoke in him surprise and joy, but also fear and pain. It is the sound of music that draws him initially to a Salvation Army band, a group whose line he quickly joins, adding to their harmonies his own happy mimicry. The youngest female member of the group drags him along to share pizza with the group and then promptly takes him to bed. The next morning, he goes in search of food and is yelled at by a treelopper (Jip de Heer), helped by a wealthy woman (Celine O'Leary), beaten by a policeman and finally rescued by an alternative punk-rock band, who take him along on their tour. Travelling with the band in the back of their open-roof truck, Bubby is entranced by their improvised music. He acts as the band's apprentice-roadie until the stench of the dead cat he is still carrying in

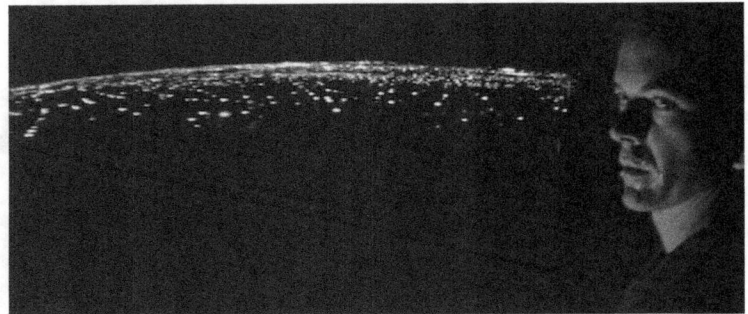
Figure 2: Bubby sees the world for the first time.

his suitcase, and his smiling declaration that the murdered man and woman on the front page of the local newspaper are his Mom and Pop, alert them to the fact that their mascot is the now infamous 'cling wrap killer'. For their own protection – and his – the band leave Bubby with an associate, guru-like gallery owner Dan (Bruce Gilbert), who gives him new clothes and a new hairstyle.

In his new attire, Bubby almost passes as 'normal'. At a bar, listening to music with Dan, Bubby becomes enchanted by a woman, the aptly named Angel (Carmel Johnson). He approaches her but his uninhibited declaration of: 'You've got great tits, great big whoppers', sends the plump Angel running from the bar. Bubby catches up with her on the street and grabs her breast, just as he previously would have his mother's. She screams and in the next scene we see Bubby, handcuffed, being led into a police station.

In a prison cell somewhat reminiscent of his home, Bubby regresses to his previous behaviour as, on all fours, he catches and dismembers cockroaches. The perverse, night-duty cop begs Bubby to talk to him. But Bubby ignores him, preoccupied with his cockroaches. When he hears the unexpected and soulful sounds of bagpipes being played by the police band, he makes a racket trying to escape his confines. The night-duty cop drags him from the cell and forces him into a faeces-smeared confinement block where a muscular, naked male prisoner crouches in a corner. When Bubby introduces himself as the 'cling wrap killer', 'the Animal' stands up, forces Bubby onto his stomach and rapes him.

Released from prison, Bubby again wanders the streets until the sound of organ music draws him into the partially demolished interior of a church. Here he meets the organ-playing scientist (Norman Kaye), whose sermon on the need to 'think God out of existence' finally helps to disabuse Bubby of his fear of an almighty being. In his next random encounter he sees a group of women going upstairs into a building. One of them (Michelle O'Regan) reminds him of his mother so he waits for her. When she reappears, he gleefully says hello and grabs her breasts. The women turn on him and, pushing him to the ground, repeatedly kick him. Bruised and beaten, he returns to his bunker-like home, where it becomes apparent that he doesn't really understand the finality of death. Lying in the white lines that trace the shape of his murdered mother's body, Bubby cries himself to sleep, and we begin to understand the complexity of their relationship. On awakening, he dresses in his father's clothes and again attempts to confront the world, but this time in the adult form of Pop.

Bubby takes to sleeping in a junk pile on Port Adelaide's industrial wharfs. He adopts a stray kitten and begins to understand the consequences of his actions. He goes in search of food and instead stumbles across the band, joyously joining them on stage. Mesmerised by his front-of-stage position, Bubby begins a litany of mimicry, abuse and sexually explicit soundbites, all intercut with hisses and growls. He is an instant hit with the alternative crowd. The band members don't want Bubby to leave, but he insists on returning to the wharf to take care of his kitten. Returning to the junk pile, he finds some young thugs have tortured his pet to death. The next day we find him in a park, eating pizza and stroking his dead cat. Here he again encounters Angel, who is a carer for a group of people with cerebral palsy. Miraculously, Bubby can understand their speech. They take him in and Bubby forms a special relationship with Rachael (Rachael Huddy), whose speech he translates for the benefit of Angel and the other carers (Maryla Galus and Janet Kanda). Rachael develops feelings for Bubby, but he, in turn, has fallen in love with

Angel and they begin a relationship. Bubby continues to live in the centre, but every night he joins the band on stage, his central performance a cathartic re-enactment of the trauma of his entrapment, the abuse he has suffered and his sexual relations with his large-breasted mother, now transformed into a loving relationship with Angel.

Angel invites Bubby to lunch with her pious and bigoted parents. Their abuse of their daughter upsets Bubby, whom we see in the next scene wandering around a junk pile, collecting scraps of cling wrap – an indication of his murderous intent. We move from Bubby and Angel standing under a glorious, enveloping sky discussing the death of Angel's parents, to one of the band members lecturing Bubby that he mustn't kill any more people. On stage that night Bubby undertakes one of his wildest performances, facilitated by a blow-up sex doll with enormous breasts. The band members accompany him; with their heads encased in masks of cling wrap, they bear an uncanny resemblance to Bubby's murder victims while also seeming otherworldly. In quick succession, we then see Bubby and Angel engaging in tender sex on an altar-like table, followed by Angel giving birth, while Bubby already holds another swaddled child. The film concludes with a tracking shot through an industrial area that finds Bubby in a scene of domestic bliss, running around the front yard of a house littered with swings and toys, playing with his two small children, while Angel sits on a swing, stroking a new kitten.

# ✖ PART 1

## SOMEWHERE BETWEEN EXPLOITATION AND ART CINEMA

## A Brief History

Rolf de Heer arrived in Sydney, Australia in 1959 as an eight-year-old boy who didn't 'know a word of English' (quoted in de Heer, 2008, p. 115). He was born in Heemskerk in the Netherlands and migrated to Australia with his family after several years living in Sumatra (Starrs, 2009, p. 1). As an invited contributor to the 2008 collection *Australian Greats*, he reminisced: 'I learnt my new language quickly, almost revelled in it. I read voraciously, forgot my Dutch and within a couple of years English was my best subject' (p. 115). These days this 'immigrant' is considered a veteran of the Australian cinema. Nationally and internationally, he is best known for his two award-winning films, *The Tracker* and *Ten Canoes*, both of which deal with indigenous issues. Set in 1922 in the Australian outback, *The Tracker* delivers up a confrontational and shameful narrative of the brutalities that white settlers inflicted on the indigenous population. The story was born out of de Heer's interest in early Australian colonial history ('Production Notes', Vertigo Productions, 1985). The film's stunning use of light and the rich colours of the land become the stage for a tragedy of classical proportions, played out through the iconic figures of the Tracker (David Gulpilil), the Follower (Damon Gameau), the Fugitive (Noel Wilton) and the Fanatic (Gary Sweet). The film follows the four figures' travels through the relentless landscape, yet the audience is never given a firm sense of the purpose of the quest, or the personal history of the ensemble. De Heer invited the legendary indigenous actor Gulpilil, whom he considers 'emblematic of the performance area of black Australia' ('Production Notes', Vertigo Productions, 1985), to play the role of the Tracker. Although working for the white authorities, Gulpilil's character is a trickster figure. Brutalised by the Fanatic, he eventually outplays him in a stunning reversal of colonial history.

Taking us back into mythic time, *Ten Canoes* presents a lush and bountiful world inhabited by the indigenous people of Gunalbingu. It also tells a story about the old ways, highlighting tribal practices such as hunting and gathering food and the making of crafts. Like *The Tracker*, the film circulated extensively on the film festival circuit and won numerous awards, including the Special Jury Prize, Un Certain Regard, at the Cannes Film Festival in May 2006 ('Festivals and Awards', Vertigo Productions, 1985). Shot in and around the Arafura swap in North-east Arnhem Land in the Northern Territory of Australia, the film is a tragicomedy of lust and revenge. The cast is made up of Gunalbingu and other related clan members with Gulpilil delivering the English-language voiceover while his son, Jamie, plays the role of a young man who covets the wife of another. The film is unique in that it is the first feature shot in an Aboriginal language.

Made more than a decade after *Bad Boy Bubby*, these mature works of an established and esteemed film-maker have a very different history from this earlier production. Yet the way in which de Heer's idea for *Bad Boy Bubby* evolved does have a correlation with many low-budget films – a slow cultivation, meshed together in snatched moments of downtime. From 1970, the director worked at the Australian Broadcasting Commission undertaking various jobs including stints as a film librarian, a film editing assistant, a programme assessor and a publicity officer. In 1977, tired of working on other directors' projects, he applied and was accepted into the Australian Film and TV School, completing his Diploma of Film and TV in Production and Directing in 1980. Aged thirty-two, he was one of six who graduated in directing. The award-winning editor, Suresh Ayyar, who worked on *Bad Boy Bubby*, graduated the same year (Starrs, 2009, p. 9).

De Heer's first film was the children's feature *Tail of a Tiger* (1984), a wondrous but unchallenging story about Orville Ryan (Grant Navin), a twelve-year-old misfit obsessed with flying and fascinated by Tiger Moth biplanes. The project came to de Heer through the Producers' Circle in Sydney, which had asked him to write a documentary script about the enthusiasts restoring the wreck of one of these planes. While working on the script, de Heer recognised the potential of the source material, adapting it into a fictional story that would 'appeal to children of all ages, from five to ninety-five' ('Press Kit Notes', Vertigo Productions, 1985). The film was both critically and commercially successful; in 1985, it screened in the Official Selection for Kinderfest at the Berlin Film Festival and it also won Second Prize for Feature Length, Live Action Film at the Chicago International Film Festival of Children's Films.

Set in an isolated homestead where electricity seems to have taken on a life of its own and neighbours have begun to mysteriously disappear, *Incident at Raven's Gate* (1987), de Heer's second feature, is an unpredictable and atmospheric science-fiction thriller. In his discussion of Australian national cinema, Tom O'Regan asserts that the industry's typically smaller budgets limit its capacity to produce stage spectacle, resulting in a reliance on dialogue – of 'telling as much as showing' – culminating in a cinema that is more 'sociologically and people reliant' (1996, p. 262). Even when working in genres such as science fiction, O'Regan argues that Australian cinema's creative approach to budget limitations has been to focus less on the spectacle of 'machines, objects and viruses' than on the effect of these 'sometimes unseen monsters on an *interpersonal* rather than *public* scale'. Including de Heer's *Incident at Raven's Gate* in his discussion, O'Regan says 'the alien force that kills and transforms people into zombies affects a handful of characters whose relationships with each other are important'. He further contends that the '*paranoid* qualities of Australian cinema owe as much to limited production horizons as to any Australian propensity to paranoia' (1996, p. 262).

Beginning work in the decade after the release of the high-concept blockbuster *Jaws* (1975) meant that de Heer entered a domestic industry unable to compete with the audience appeal of established Hollywood big-budget spectacles. De Heer, however, sees low-budget productions as both creatively enabling and an economic restriction he must work around:

> I'm sort of schizophrenic about the question of how directors get to say what they want to say; I've learnt to apply an opportunistic and

> mathematical mode of thinking to the ideals and preoccupations of my work. I can talk about my projects as utter contrivances in the most commercially cynical fashion imaginable, while at the same time not care a jot for the market and be completely passionate about the content, the process and the people I'm working with. (quoted in Caputo and Burton, 2002, p. 50)

In a low-budget film such as *Incident at Raven's Gate*, de Heer manages to impart an uneasy sense of foreboding. While more than double the budget of *Bad Boy Bubby*, *Incident at Raven's Gate*'s cost of AUD2.5 million is still meagre. Discussing low-budget film-making in an interview in 2002, de Heer commented: 'I can't compete with the likes of, say, *The Mummy II* (2001) or *Lara Croft: Tomb Raider* (2001), but I can provide an experience that is different' (quoted in Caputo and Burton, 2002, p. 54). Interestingly, in an interview conducted in 1994 when de Heer won the Australian Film Institute (AFI) Awards for both the script and direction of *Bad Boy Bubby*, he commented that Australian film-making was having a good year. The 'FFC [Film Finance Corporation] was obviously getting it right ... Australian culture was somehow contributing and so, too, might be the failures of the 10BA films of the 1980s' (quoted in George, 1994, p. 6). The 1980s period de Heer alludes to is a complex decade in the history of a national film industry attempting not only to establish itself, but also to encourage the international exhibition of Australian films. The now legendary 10BA was a tax concession introduced by the Australian government to facilitate private investment in Australian film and television productions. While this is not the place to discuss the pros and cons of this tax break, it is worth contextualizing the director's reference to the concession. The industry exemption was given the title of the Division 10BA; a part of the Income Tax Assessment Amendment Bill that revised the previous Income Tax Assessment Act of 1936 and became law on 24 June 1981 (Beilby and Lansell, 1983, pp. 160–1). The exemption led to a boom in feature-film production, which more than doubled from 1981 to 1985. Yet with the increase in productions came an increase in costs, with budgets tripling, and studio and legal costs continually rising (Dermody and Jacka, 1987, p. 67). The exponential growth in demand meant that directors, crews and actors could also demand much higher pay. The FFC modified the Division 10BA in 1988 and, while the period gave rise to the 'new wave' of Australian cinema, it also resulted in inflated costs, a backlog of productions and abuses of the system to the point where, at some stages in the decade, films did not have to make it to the cinema or onto VHS video for investors to receive their money. They just had to be made (Dermody and Jacka, 1987, p. 5).

De Heer's desire to work in a low-budget sector, for both financial and artistic reasons, can be appreciated against the backdrop of the Hollywood blockbuster and in the context of the abuses of the 10BA, with its ramifications for the industry. However, the director also believes that working in that sector grants him the freedom to maintain a sense of difference – a difference which has ensured his longevity as one of the few contemporary, visionary directors of the Australian cinema. This singular vision is again found in the Australian and French co-production, *Dingo* (1991), which was de Heer's next venture, and is infamous as the only film in which the legendary jazz musician, Miles Davis, ever made an appearance. Travelling from outback Western Australia to the clubs of Paris, the film is a musical odyssey that traces the story of the naive John 'Dingo' Anderson (Colin Friels), and his dream to play trumpet with the great jazz legend Billy Cross (Miles Davis). At the AFI Awards in 1991, *Dingo* notched up seven nominations, including those for Best Film and Best Director, and it won for Best Sound and Best Music. At the Asia Pacific Film Festival in 1992, the film picked up an award for Best Music.

On the surface, no trace of the controversial nature of *Bad Boy Bubby* is discernible in de Heer's first three films, preoccupied as they are with fantasy and dreams; the only possible thread seems to be a fascination with childhood. While there are hints of a darker sensibility in the brooding atmosphere of *Incident at Raven's Gate*, it is hard to find any identifiable visual style presaging the bleak and sometimes surreal aesthetics of *Bad Boy Bubby*. De Heer has strong opinions about the significance of the different elements of creating a film. 'Writing, producing and directing', he says, 'are quite often treated as separate strands of the film making process, though for me they are completely interdependent and I think some of the most profound creative decisions are made by producers' (quoted in Caputo and Burton, 2002, p. 48). In the last century, a characteristic of the Australian cinema has often been identified as the writer and director – the auteur who, through input at numerous levels of the film-making process, has contributed to a singular, identifiable vision of cinema, with particular funding outcomes (Rayner, 2000, p. 121). De Heer fits this category; he works in a way that is aligned with the 'European brand of art-film auteurism based on personal writing and visual expressions' (Rayner, 2000, p. 12). He is adamant that the director must be involved in the writing process and this explains some of the difficulties he faced during the making of *Dingo*, on which he was the director and producer, with Marc Rosenberg as the writer and co-producer. Close friends who met at film school, de Heer and Rosenberg first worked together on *Incident at Raven's Gate*, but the strain of making *Dingo* led to a rift (Susskind, 1994, p. 81). Of his experiences working on another writer's script, de Heer comments:

> One of my problems on *Dingo* (1991) was that although I loved the script, in the first half of the shoot I tried to realize someone else's vision. I didn't, even simply as a director, attempt to make my own vision because I was quite close to the scriptwriter Marc Rosenberg, and I knew how important the script was to him. It was a very difficult situation I got myself into, and that is why I'm quite reluctant now to direct someone else's script unless I can make it according to my own vision. (quoted in Caputo and Burton, 2002, p. 48)

Born out of his experience with *Dingo*, de Heer saw *Bad Boy Bubby* as a project that would allow him complete freedom to write and direct a creation of his own. The industrial context of his choice to make a low-budget production further ensured a lack of interference with the project, culminating in the freedom to produce something 'different' (quoted in Pearce, 1994, p. 14) – a desire that de Heer has held on to throughout his working career.

De Heer's process of developing the idea for a film is an interesting one. The screenplay for *Bad Boy Bubby* came together over many years. The director's practice involves the use of cards on which he collects ideas, jokes, insights, bits of stories, opinions and occurrences, which he then pins to a wall where he is working, or living, until he reaches a point at which he can see the whole screenplay. He then puts it down on paper in an 'intense session usually lasting between one and three weeks' (de Heer, 1996, p. 7). For a decade, *Bad Boy Bubby* was little more than a collection of ideas on a number of cards. The impetus for the project came about directly after de Heer left film school and wanted to make his own film. Of course, no one was willing to invest in an untried director, fresh out of film school, with no available resources. So, while working on other people's projects, de Heer began to plan a film that he would shoot on weekends, with a friend's 35mm camera, and any money he made during the week would go towards buying film stock. The process of shooting on weekends would inevitably extend the production period, possibly to at least two years. At this point, he realized that no single crew would be continuously available over this period of time, particularly not a cinematographer. His inventive response to this problem was to decide that each scene could be shot by a different cinematographer. Furthermore, the advantage of setting the opening act in a confined room without newspapers, television or radio was that the film would not be instantly dated by its drawn-out production (quoted in Caputo and Burton, 2002, p. 52). De Heer stayed true to both decisions when he finally came to make the film, restricting the first half-hour to one room and using thirty-one cinematographers to capture Bubby's episodic experience of the unknown outside world.

With several productions behind him and approximately ten years after leaving film school, de Heer felt in a better position to make a film – and that it was something he needed to do. Sifting through his piles of cards, he concluded that *Bubby* – the film's original title – was the most realized of his different projects:

> A few weeks later, after one of the most enjoyable writing experiences I've had, there was a first draft. It was a draft that spoke very strongly to the reader (provoking vitriol mixed equally with praise and a lot of very strange looks at me as a person), and suddenly it was a project, a real project with strong prospects of being financed. (de Heer, 1996, p. 8)

From then on, de Heer claims the project proceeded very quickly, with every scene of the original screenplay being filmed except one small section that was subject to rewrites (de Heer, 1996, p. 8). At this time, de Heer was living in South Australia and the state government initially provided funds to help him complete his script and to develop the project to the point at which it could secure principal investors (Morris, 1993). Having completed the script, de Heer felt that it spoke 'loudly' and had something powerful to say. Through his connection with prolific composer Michel Legrand, who worked with Miles Davis to compose the soundtrack for *Dingo*, the script was sent to the Italian producer, Domenico Procacci. At a time when Australian features were rarely made for under AUD2 million, Procacci promptly committed to half of the AUD880,000 budget.

At this point de Heer considered that, as a marketable product, there were several possibilities for *Bad Boy Bubby*: 'At worst, you stick a lurid cover on it and stick it out on video and it will get some sort of exploitation returns …. At best, it could get a lot more, which it did' (2010b). With Procacci's Italian company Fandango having committed to half the budget, the AFC (Australian Film Commission) agreed to furnish the other half. Procacci went on to either produce or act as executive producer on all of de Heer's subsequent films. In 2002, he established an arm of his Fandango company in Sydney, Australia, with de Heer and fellow Australian cinema identities, director Richard Lowenstein, producer Sue Murray and director and lawyer Bryce Menzies. *Bad Boy Bubby* appears to be the initial inspiration for Procacci's habit of fostering notorious and often low-budget productions. In 2011 the producer again courted controversy as the co-producer of *Diaz – Don't Clean Up This Blood* (2012), a film that tackles the infamous police brutality against anti-globalization protesters at the 2001 summit in Genoa (Vivarelli, 2011).

## Casting

Having secured funding for the film's production, for de Heer, the casting of its main character was crucial. A fascination with the innocence of childhood and the notion of innocence in danger has driven many of the director's projects, as has the idea of innocence found through redemption. Bubby is literally a baby, newborn to the world, yet the brutality and dark side of selfhood explored by the film meant that it was impossible to cast a child in the part. Bubby had to be played by an adult, but one who could capture the innocence and curiosity of childhood. Nicholas Hope's performance as Bubby is nothing short of astounding, but he was not the director's first choice. Part of the original inspiration for *Bad Boy Bubby* was born out of de Heer's desire to make a film with an actor friend, Ritchie Singer, who at the time was a student at NIDA (National Institute of Dramatic Arts). De Heer was greatly affected by seeing the young Singer's portrayal of a seventy-year-old man, Dodge, a character from Sam Shepard's Pulitzer Prize-winning play, *Buried Child* (1978). Singer played one of the main characters, Richard, in *Incident at Raven's Gate*, and while the Sydney actor pulled out of the project in 1992, his performance of Dodge was, in part, the inspiration for the character of Pop, who was played in *Bad Boy Bubby* by veteran Australian actor Ralph Cotterill (Malone, 2001b, p. 59). Hope secured the role of Bubby after de Heer remembered seeing him in a short film called *The Confessor Caresser* (1989), in which he played a 'wannabe' serial killer (Fitzgerald, 1994, p. 38). (The short is now included in the special features on the 2005 DVD release and the 2010 Blu-ray release of *Bad Boy Bubby* by Umbrella).

Originally from Manchester, Hope came to Australia with his family in 1966 when he was seven. He became interested in acting relatively late and at twenty-six enrolled to study at Flinders University Drama Centre. He was also a member of the South Australian youth theatre ensemble, the Magpie Theatre Company, for two years (Daly, 1994, p. 12). In his 2004 autobiography *Brushing the Tip of Fame*, he describes how the film affected his life. As the main protagonist of a production that he terms a 'cult hit', his life was turned upside-down (p. 4). After the film first screened in competition in Venice, the 'novice star was mobbed on the streets for autographs and feted by the likes of director James Ivory (*Howards End*, 1992), who told Hope his performance was "absolutely brilliant"' (Fitzgerald, 1994, p. 380). Nevertheless, despite the acclaim, in between jetting from festival to festival, Hope struggled to find work and remained on unemployment benefits just to pay his rent (Hope, 2004, p. 113). While Hope, as Bubby, is in every scene and our perspective is most often his point of view, there are three other key roles in the film. The extraordinary role of Mom (Florence or Flo as she is referred to by Pop), was played by the courageous Claire Benito, who has since died of cancer. While Benito occasionally worked in film and television, she mainly acted in the theatre. As previously mentioned, de Heer cast Ralph Cotterill as Pop, while Carmel Johnson played Angel. Johnson's last film performance was in Phillip Noyce's *Rabbit Proof Fence* (2002). The rest of the cast consisted of friends, relations, members of the local film and music scene and volunteers – specifically for the club scenes when Bubby and the band perform. While the set was mostly a harmonious place, the director has commented that Benito was an instinctive actor who was sometimes driven crazy by Cotterill's text-based methods and his insistence on repeatedly rehearsing their scenes (2010a).

## The Shoot: Cinematic Experimentation

A low-budget film, *Bad Boy Bubby* was shot in nine weeks in Port Adelaide, South Australia. Shooting began on 16 November 1992, ran for five weeks, stopped for a two-week break over Christmas and then continued in the summer of 1993 for another four weeks (Hope, 2004, p. 16). The intense schedule involved working twelve-hour days (Susskind, 1994, p. 81). Two weeks before the shoot began: 'We just locked ourselves in a room', notes Hope, who improvised his actions in every scene and developed Bubby's 'gangly' walk from studying videos on autism. For Hope, Bubby was a character more intelligent than his environment would ever allow him to be (Fitzgerald, 1994, p. 38). To help Hope with his character's seamless repetition of everything he hears around him – human, animal, even mechanical sounds, in a form of echolalia – De Heer shot in sequence to enable the actor to know what he was supposed to copy. This choice further informs the sense of the film being entirely from Bubby's perspective; yet the director's idea to use binaural microphones works to further increase the audience's identification with Bubby. As Anna Hicky-Moody and Melissa Iocco note, the effect of the binaural microphones (see below) is to provoke 'a corporeal response' (2004, p. 78).

As previously mentioned, thirty-one different cinematographers were engaged to chronicle the adventures of this man-child, one purpose being to effect a sense of 'seeing the world for the first time' (de Heer, 2010a). In the credits under the title, 'Camera: Contributing Cinematographers in order of appearance', is a list of thirty-one names with the primary director of photography, Ian Jones at the top. The fact that footage was shot by thirty-one cinematographers, each (except for Jones) unable to refer to the work of the others, and the use of binaural microphones represent further evidence of the experimental way in which the film was conceived and shot. Several articles and chapters have been devoted to exploring the film in the context of its sound, which is considered by some practitioners to be an extraordinary experiment in film-making (Cat Hope, 2004; Hicky-Moody and Iocco, 2004; Starrs, 2010). Long-time collaborator, sound designer James Currie, helped develop a binaural headset for Hope to wear under the wig that is part of Bubby's costume. Initially trying to work with Sony radio mikes, de Heer and Currie were eventually put in contact with Frederick Stahl – an 'extraordinary character' who worked for the Australian Security Intelligence Organization (ASIO) building tiny transmitters (de Heer quoted by Pearce, 1994, p. 14). Stahl and his wife, Margaret, constructed the device and Stahl agreed to stay and work on the film. He loved the experience and kept improving and fixing his device. Reminiscing about the shoot, de Heer affectionately notes that 'Fred' spent much of his time standing at the 'side of Nick's head with a screwdriver' (quoted in Pearce, 1994, p.14). Stahl went on to work with Heather Rose, an actor with cerebral palsy, in the film she starred in and wrote with de Heer, *Dance Me to My Song* (1998). Rose, who died in 2002, was confined to a wheelchair and spoke with the aid of a computer and voicebox. Her appearance in *Bad Boy Bubby* in 1998 may have been uncredited but she went on to receive a standing ovation at the Cannes Film Festival and rave reviews for her performance as Julie in *Dance Me to My Song* (Stahl, 2002). Stahl's binaural microphones captured her ragged breathing, which then became the bedrock for the soundtrack of the film.

The binaural microphones, D. Bruno Starrs notes, position the listener between the two of them – in the case of *Bad Boy Bubby*, 'virtually between Bubby's ears' – we are positioned in his sonic journey, resulting in a kind of magnification (2010, p. 33). The sonic focus of the sound changes according to the movement of the actor's head, but it also means that we hear his body, his breathing and the intimate recording of his voice (Cat Hope, 2004). Starrs offers an interesting insight into de Heer's stylistic choice:

> In *Bad Boy Bubby* writer/director de Heer used sound to demarcate the two distinctly different worlds: the hellhole of Flo's dank and dirty apartment and the marvel of the unexplored universe outside. The disjointed, minimalist dialogue between Flo and Bubby is embedded in a claustrophobic, industrial, almost metallic soundscape … . These deadening, uninspiring aural circumstances, entirely devoid of music, are soon left behind. Once freed, Bubby experiences an astonishing series of growth-enhancing meetings with sound and music, from his initial encounter with a Salvation Army choir he hears from afar and compulsively seeks out to the barking of an aggressive Alsatian dog. The second part of the film is richly saturated with diegetic and non-diegetic music and sound. (Starrs, 2010, pp. 33–4)

The director made a number of other interesting choices during the shoot. Shortly after the film's release, de Heer talked with David Pearce in *Movie Trader* about how he views the film as an exploration of 'what is cinema and what is cinematic' (1994, p. 14). At the time de Heer was making *Bad Boy Bubby*, his attitude to television was somewhat negative, for he believed that the cinema offered bolder and more adventurous possibilities. One of these possibilities is widescreen, which de Heer had previously used in *Incident at Raven's Gate* and *Dingo*. But, as Pearce notes, widescreen is not what you expect from a film that spends its first act in a dingy, small hovel. De Heer sheds some light on the history of this stylistic preference:

> [M]y first idea was to have the opening section in 1:1.33 and then as [Bubby] walks through the door outside, the doorframe would be contained in the 1.33 frame until you move closer and closer, until it meets the edges of the frame and then, as he continues to move through, the whole screen opens up into widescreen. And that seemed like a very good idea ... for quite a way into the cut, every time we screened it, we would mask it at the beginning and then pull the masks away when he went out. But that opening section which is pretty gruelling as it is, was unbearable in 1.33 – it was disassociating, too, it was much more distanced from the audience, but it was just so unpleasant, that I don't think I could recover from that in terms of seeing the whole film. Then, one day, we took the masking away from the opening and it was like a revelation to me, it worked fundamentally differently as a film. (quoted in Pearce, 1994, p. 14)

It is easy to imagine how the 1.33 aspect ratio of 16mm film, also common in television and video, would seem like an appropriate stylistic choice. Its intimate effect would further compound the sense of Bubby's entrapment. However, it is just as easy to imagine that the claustrophobic elements of the opening sequence would become relentless over its length to the point of being, as de Heer has noted, 'unbearable'.

There are two other points of stylistic interest that de Heer discusses on the Audio Commentary to the 2005 DVD release by Umbrella, which also appears on the 2010 Blu-ray release. The first was a conscious decision to have the set for the first act expand by 50 per cent when Pop enters Bubby's world. The set was built to a certain size, but when the door opens and Pop enters the apartment/dungeon, the space has doubled. It is as if with Pop's entrance into Bubby's world, his horizons expand and his universe increases. The other decision was to include footage in the final cut that was accidentally produced due to faulty equipment. De Heer discovered that footage shot of the scene in the first act when Pop and Mom arrive home drunk was distorted. The 'lens hadn't been seated properly', producing a skewed and twisted image of Bubby's mother and father (see Figure 3). In one of those serendipitous moments, de Heer decided to retain the footage in the final cut as it seemed to conjure a number of appropriate sensations, including the blurred vision of drunkenness and Bubby's confusion in perceiving his parents' inebriation, while not really understanding their changed demeanour. It may also hint at the murderous rage building within the protagonist.

Figure 3: Distorted image of Mom and Pop's drunken return.

## Festival Fame and the OCIC Award

Seven months after *Bad Boy Bubby* was completed, de Heer, feeling he had 'something' but not quite sure what, sent the film, 'on a whim and a prayer', to the 1993 Venice Film Festival. To his surprise and delight, it was accepted into competition at what was the 50th Venice Film Festival, the second one directed by Gillo Pontecorvo. Hope, the sound designer Currie and the director all travelled to Venice where they met with the producer Procacci. They were completely unknown, they had no expectations, but the film 'tore the place down' (de Heer, 2010b). It became a phenomenon, an award-winning film – yet its festival success and its eventual release were tinged with controversy.

De Heer, Hope and Currie have described in numerous publications the extraordinary experience of having a film in competition in Venice, and the overwhelming response they received from the critics and at public screenings. Interestingly, their comments and recollections of the critics' screening vary wildly. In an interview with Anne Susskind of *HQ* magazine, Currie comments that the three of them were drinking outside the cinema on the afternoon of the screening. Their hearts sank when they saw one of the critics leave the theatre, before Procacci appeared to tell them that maybe thirty or forty critics were in attendance. Currie notes that in response to his comments, Rolf and Nick turned white: '30 or 40 out of 2000 critics is a terrible showing'. Procacci then smiled and said: 'It was a packed house .... They loved it' (Currie quoted by Susskind, 1994, p. 79). Hope's recollections of that afternoon are somewhat different. In his autobiography, published nearly ten years after the event, he recalls that they attended the screening, the cinema was only three-quarters full and a small part of the audience stood up as if to leave during the sequence in which Bubby torments the cat. They ended up staying and at the conclusion of the film, the critics gave them a standing ovation (Hope, 2004, pp. 45–6). Their memories of the screening for the public, however, are similar.

The 50th Venice Film Festival was one of pomp, ceremony and spectacle. Red carpet was laid from the Excelsior, the festival hotel, to the main competition cinema. There were TV cameras and spotlights, huge crowds and security guards leading the way to the cinema. The public screening occurs directly after the critics' screening in an adjacent cinema that holds more than 1,000. At the public screening de Heer, Currie and Hope were led up to the front row of the balcony. Even after the success of the critics' screening, they were still a little terrified. Festival audiences can be tough and, at Venice, if the public dislikes a film, they whistle (Currie quoted by Susskind, 1994, p. 80). As Australians, the three of them were acutely aware of this possibility because at the 1989 festival it had happened to an Australian film – New Zealand director Jane Campion's *Sweetie* (1989). While in later years *Sweetie*'s critical reputation has been reassessed, its initial screenings divided festival audiences across the world. European critics expressed disgust at the 'psychologically deranged' and overweight title character Sweetie's (Geneviève Lemon) transgression of the supposed norms of femininity (Pullar, 2006). Although Campion has since redeemed her festival reputation with the success of *An Angel at My Table* (1990) and *The Piano* (1993), Currie, de Heer and Hope remembered the negative response to *Sweetie*. At its public screening in Venice, the crowd had shown their disapproval by whistling while a lukewarm reception from critics to a screening at the Cannes Festival had sent Campion running from the theatre 'in tears' (Malcolm, 1993). While Currie has described the public screening as chaotic and nerve-wracking, with people talking and coming and going, no such fate awaited *Bad Boy Bubby* (quoted in Susskind, 1994, p. 80). When the credits finally rolled, there was silence before their names were called and they were invited to stand. The public audience started to applaud, but went completely wild when Hope stood up. From then on, everywhere they went people clapped, stamped their feet, 'girls kissed them and boys asked for autographs' (Hope, 2004, pp. 46–9).

The critics' appreciation of *Bad Boy Bubby* at the Venice Film Festival was nothing short of adulatory; de Heer's film is repeatedly described as unconventional, offensive yet extraordinary. It is one of the few films out of the hundreds screened at the festival that is mentioned in most reviews. Enthusiastic responses were elicited from a broad range of significant news publications such as *Le Monde*, the *Guardian* and the *Economist*. Writing for *The Times* (London), David Robinson's sentiments about the film are fairly typical of the tone of most reviews:

> The festival's *enfant terrible* was the Dutch-Australian director Rolf de Heer, whose mischievous *Bad Boy Bubby* took the special prize of the jury. The film displays the admirable Australian capacity for disregarding all accepted conventions of taste. (1993)

Similarly the *Economist* notes that the 'real triumph' of the festival was de Heer's *Bad Boy Bubby*:

> The film examines deprivation, innocence and immorality through an adult-aged but child-minded character called Bubby, who is played with great originality by Nick Hope … . Film Festivals are in part about the discovery of new art-house directors who have the potential to reach their audiences. Mr de Heer's powerful insight into the mind of an 'adult' coming to terms with his own massively stunted growth is a case in point. It deserves to win a place on cinema screens across the world. (Anonymous, 1993, p. 96)

Writing for the American film journal *Film Comment*, European editor Harlan Kennedy suggests that:

> Director de Heer wouldn't recognize good taste if it fell off a tall building and brained him. But *Bad Boy Bubby*'s bad taste offers something richer: a horror-comic delight in primal story colors and a *Candide*-like logic in showing the effects of runaway innocence on a defenseless world. (1993, p. 65)

At the Venice Film Festival, the film won an array of awards including the Grand Special Jury Prize; the FIPRESCI (International Critics) Award, shared with Robert Altman's *Short Cuts* (1993); Italian Cinemagoers Award (CIAK) for Best Film and Best Actor; and it won the OCIC (Ecumenical Award) Bronze Plaque.

Before moving on to a discussion of how the film was classified and distributed, one can't help but ask: why was *Bad Boy Bubby*, with its blasphemy, incest and physical abuse, ever even considered by the OCIC (International Catholic Organization for Cinema) for an ecumenical prize, let alone awarded a Bronze Plaque? Possibly this question reveals more about preconceived ideas of what sort of media might be valued by religious organizations than it does about the organizations themselves. A certain bias exists around perceptions of films that typically win ecumenical awards, yet a quick glance at the list of winners for the last twenty-five years or so reveals a diverse and fascinating collection of OCIC award recipients. Rainer Werner Fassbinder's *Angst essen Seele auf* (*Ali: Fear Eats the Soul*) and Francis Ford Coppola's *The Conversation* were the first films to win at Cannes in 1974. Andrei Tarkovsky has won at Cannes on numerous occasions with *Staker* in 1980, *Nostaligis* in 1983 and *The Sacrifice* in 1986. In 1981, Ken Loach was awarded at Cannes for *Looks and Smiles* and again in 1990 for *Hidden Agenda*; he also won in Berlin in 1994 with *Ladybird, Ladybird*. Atom Egoyan's *Family Viewing* picked up the prize in Locarno in 1988 and *The Sweet Hereafter* won in Cannes in 1997. Bryan McKenzie's *With Love to the Person Next to Me* received the award in Locarno in 1987 and Lee Tamahori won in Montreal in 1994 with *Once Were Warriors*.

The OCIC and the International Catholic Organization for Radio and Television (UNDA) became a united organization called SIGNIS (World Catholic Association for Communication) in November 2001. Father Peter Malone, who was the president of SIGNIS from 2002–9 and is a member of the Pontifical Council for social communications, has remarked on numerous occasions how important it is for the church to 'engage with the world of popular and serious cinema' (2001). His website of film reviews is evidence of this sentiment, showing a 'catholic' taste when it comes to choice of subjects. His reviews, such as the one for *Bad Boy Bubby*, treat films as teaching texts through which questions are posed to encourage discussion around a Christian reading (SIGNIS: World Catholic Association for Communications website). OCIC and Interfilm have also published summarized criteria for judging films for their awards:

1. The film must be of a high artistic quality.
2. The film must have positive human values.
3. The values presented in the film can be seen in light of the message of the gospel.
4. The film challenges its audience to respond to its social and justice dimensions and can be used with groups to understand issues through story and symbols it proposes.
5. The film reflects its culture, helping its audience to respect the language and images of that culture.
6. The film has a universal impact and is not confined to its national or local context.

The awards also represent the means by which a film outside the mainstream may find distribution and a wider audience (Malone, 2001a).

Malone, who has written at length about the awards, claims there was much 'soul searching' before the OCIC jury agreed to award *Bad Boy Bubby* the Bronze Plaque, even though it breaks so many taboos. Of the lengthy debate about the film that took place among the Venice jury in 1993, Malone says that, while the majority of the members considered the film to be valid for the OCIC award, one juror described it as 'immoral'. He goes on to note that the debate around the film was 'very fruitful in highlighting the complexity of the issues raised and the relative difference in sensitivity among members of the jury' (2001a). The first prize was eventually awarded to Krzysztof Kieslowski's *Three Colours Blue* (1993), partly because some of the jury could not accept *Bad Boy Bubby* as the winner. When the film came out in Australia in 1994, while de Heer received several AFI Awards, the Australian branch of the OCIC did not even consider it for a prize. Festival juries are encouraged to give serious attention to their different sensitivities and values in measuring the scope of controversial subjects; however, in public forums some Catholic commentators went on to label *Bad Boy Bubby* 'sick' and 'indescribably bad' (Malone, 2001a).

Discussing the OCIC's decision to award *Bad Boy Bubby* the Bronze Plaque, Katie Badham observes that, pitted against *Three Colours Blue* and *Short Cuts*, the film made its mark:

> Initially the ... jury was divided with one member declaring that the film was bestial and unethical and [that they] had complained to Festival management. Some judges were fascinated by its off-beat arresting themes but found it too ugly ... . Fortunately there were some judges who argued that the breaking of new ground in theme and cinematic style and the fact that we live in a world of evil needs to be seen in films that mirror this world ... . The jury panel of theologians referred to Psalm 130, the De Profundis psalm, 'Out of the depths, I cry to you' in their description of 'Bad Boy Bubby'. This was indeed apt. It is a film that takes its audience into the depths of brutality and the ugliness of human experience yet it reaches out in hope of finding meaning for the experience. (1993)

Malone has further elaborated on the use of the Psalms to examine *Bad Boy Bubby* as *De Profundis*:

> Such a film shows the human condition in all its ugliness and desperation: men and women crying out in agony without knowing whether anyone, human or divine, can hear their voice. ... This is the world of *Mean Streets* or *Taxi Driver*, of *Bad Lieutenant* or *The Addiction*, of *Pulp Fiction* or *Very Bad Things*. Is it the world of Bergman, Fellini, Bunuel or Almodovar? Do ecumenical juries need to have experiences of these 'de profundis' films which may deserve to be winners of awards but which could, perhaps, 'scandalise' the 'faithful'?

> We have, in this post-modern era, to acknowledge that for so many individuals and societies, the absolutes have been lost while they still search for values. The post-modern collapse of the Soviet bloc serves as a mirror and as a parable for our times as do the frightening civil wars of the 90s in Africa and in the Balkans. (2001a)

While some of us would struggle to find religious sentiment within this film, the sense of Bubby as a figure in the depths of depravity, calling out to be saved, perhaps resonates with audience members who connected with and were moved by the film. Escaping his cell-like entrapment, Bubby becomes a character in search of enlightenment and salvation. While some of his murderous actions involve a sense of retribution, he is finally redeemed through acceptance, friendship and love.

*Bad Boy Bubby* went on to travel extensively on the film festival circuit, screening at twenty-nine festivals including Dei Popoli, London Film Festival, Stockholm International Film Festival in 1993, and Filmfest Hamburg, Flanders International Film Festival, International Film Festival Rotterdam and San Sebastian International Film Festival in 1994 ('Production', Screen Australia website). As late as 1998, the film screened at the Riga Film Festival in Latvia; Hope, an official guest of the Australian and French Embassies, describes the festival as 'surreal bliss' with *Bad Boy Bubby* as usual a 'popular favourite' (2004, p. 227). In 1994 at the Seattle Film Festival it won Best Achievement in Direction and Runner up Best Film. It swooped the AFI Awards by winning Best Original Screenplay, Best Achievement in Direction, Best Performance by an Actor in a Leading Role and Best Achievement in Editing. In the same year it was also awarded NSW Premier's Literary Award for Best Screenplay, yet the film never quite matched the critical success of Venice, except possibly in Australia.

At this earlier point in the film's history, we can already begin to appreciate that *Bad Boy Bubby* is a phenomenon. The film radically changed the course of Nicholas Hope's acting career and launched Rolf de Heer on the international film scene. Its peculiar conception and the experimental nature of its production would guarantee the film a following of cinema enthusiasts, academics and film buffs. However, it was its success, longevity and notoriety on the film festival circuit that ensured its status for the cinemagoing public as 'a must see film'.

# ✖ Part 2

CENSORSHIP, FILM FESTIVAL
CLASSIFICATIONS AND
PRESSURE GROUPS

*Bad Boy Bubby*'s award-winning success at the Venice Film Festival and AFI Awards was not long lived; the film soon encountered difficulties when it came to securing distribution within certain territories. More than likely, the reason the film caused little controversy at festivals is due to the laws surrounding the classification of films at this type of screening. In Australia and Britain government classification, rating and censorship boards require all films to be classified before release while in the US, it is a voluntary procedure; yet all members of the MPAA (Motion Picture Association of America) have agreed that theatrically released films should be rated. Films shown at film festivals, film events and community screenings, however, are generally exempt from these classification rulings yet, as I will discuss in the next section, these rulings are rarely straightforward.

## Classification Exemptions

The Australian Government Classification website outlines the process through which films are granted exemption. If a film has already been classified, it does not require an exemption; under the Classification Act some categories of films are 'exempt from classification due to their content'. This category includes business, accounting, professional, technical and scientific, and education films that are wholly for verification and training. Other exempt categories can include current affairs that involves news reportage and documentary recordings of sports, musical events, cultural activities and religious events. To acquire an exemption, a synopsis of the film must be submitted describing its content in relation to the 'Guidelines for the Classification of Films and Computer Games'. The guidelines request information about content that deals with themes of drug use or racism, 'implied sexual violence', 'realistically simulated sex', 'coarse language' and 'full frontal nudity'. In requesting an exemption, the festival organizers must submit a suggested classification code that correlates to the film's content. In Australia this would mean G, PG, M, MA15+, R18+. A note in bold under the 'Film Festivals and Community Screenings' section of the website states that: 'Films containing material that would exceed the classification elements corresponding to the R18+ classification (content that would cause them to be classified X18+ or RC) will not be granted a film festival exemption' (Australian Government Classification website).

The RC classification means that the film has been refused classification and, therefore, cannot be sold or screened. An X18+ classification is reserved for X-rated pornographic films containing consensual sexually explicit content, which are only legally available for sale and hire in the Northern Territory and the Australian Capital Territory. This discrepancy in the rating regulations in Australia is in part due to each state and territory possessing its own classification enforcement legislation that is complementary to the Commonwealth classification legislation. Further explanation can be found under the section 'State and Territory Government' on the Australian Government Classification website; briefly though, there are six states in Australia with their own constitutions: New South Wales, Queensland, South Australia, Tasmania, Victoria and Western Australia. The structure of the state governments mirrors that of the Australian government in that they are divided into legislature, executive and judiciary. They are permitted to pass laws 'related to any matter that is not controlled by the Commonwealth under Section 51 of the Australian Constitution'. Section 51 deals with such areas as taxation, external affairs, military defence, trade with other countries, etc. (Parliament of Australia website: Senate: Constitution). Australia is a commonwealth and the monarch's power is exercised by a Governor, while the head of the state government is called the Premier. Australia also has ten territories outside the borders of the states. The offshore territory, Norfolk Island, has been granted 'a limited right of self-government' by the Australian government. The other seven offshore territories, Ashmore and Cartier Islands, Australian Antarctic Territory, Christmas Island, Cocos (Keeling) Islands, Coral Sea Islands and Jervis Bay Territory, are governed only by Commonwealth law, usually through an Australian government-appointed administrator and deal with 'a range of governmental matters through a locally elected parliament' (Parliament of Australia website: Senate: Constitution). The only mainland territories are the Australian Capital Territory and the Northern Territory and, as their populations are significant, they are often treated as states. Relevant to our discussion are the mainland territories. Originally when the X classification was proposed in 1983, all the states and territories agreed to pass legislation enabling X-rated films to be sold to adults in their jurisdiction. However, none of the state censorship ministers followed through because of political pressure from interest groups (Vnuk, 2003). Hence, it is only in the two mainland territories that it is legal to sell X-rated films, although it is still legal to buy these films in all six states (McKee *et al.*, 2008, pp. 50–1).

An interesting case listed on the Australian Government Classification website deals with a proposed festival screening of *Ken Park* (2002), a film about the abusive domestic situation of four disenchanted, teenage skateboarders, who live in Visalia, California. The Office of Film and Literature Classification (OFLC) was responsible for classifying films, computer games and some publications until 2006.

> The OFLC received 28 complaints about the film *Ken Park* receiving an RC decision and therefore not being screened at the Sydney Film Festival in June 2003. The complaints covered a range of views on the RC decision and film festival exemption scheme. (Australian Government Classification website, pp. 42–3)

The problem, in part, occurred because the film had already been submitted for classification to the OFLC and rejected. The Sydney Film Festival Direction was issued in May 2004 by the NSW Attorney-General and applies only to the Sydney Film Festival. The direction allows the festival to show films that have, or might be, 'on the borderline of being refused classification', in addition to certain other unclassified films. The screening of these films is subject to strict conditions relating to the number of screenings, the time of the screenings and that access to the screenings is restricted to adult audiences. The complaints about the refusal to classify *Ken Park* formed part of the later stage of a letterwriting campaign that eventually resulted in the publication of 'The 2007 Film Festival Guidelines', which can be found on the Australian Government Classification website. While the document is meant only to be relevant to the Sydney Film Festival, it could serve as a blueprint for future requests by film festivals for exemptions, specifically in regard to films likely to be refused classification. In 2006 the OFLC office was closed and its responsibilities were transferred to the Classification Board, Classification Review Board and the Attorney-General's Department. While the Classification Board is responsible for classifying material, the Classification Review Board may review the former's decisions.

An entirely different controversy hit MIFF (Melbourne International Film Festival) in 2009 when Jeff Daniels's *The Ten Conditions of Love*, a documentary on the exiled Uighur leader and human-rights activist, Rebiya Kadeer, made headlines around the world. The festival director at the time, Richard Moore, decided to go public about a phone call he had received from the Chinese Consulate in Melbourne demanding that he withdraw the film from the festival. The Chinese Embassy objected to the screening as it considers Kadeer a 'terrorist'. In an interview with Lexi Metherell for *ABC*, Moore stated that he believed that the festival's website had been hacked into 'in protest about the decision to defy the Chinese Embassy and show the film on Rebiya Kadeer' (2009). The event turned into an 'international incident' with four film-makers withdrawing their Chinese-produced films, apparently in protest at the screening of the documentary. Moore suspects that the Chinese government pressured the film-makers, reporting that the festival website had been inundated with traffic and emails from China:

> We had 80,000 hits on our website on Sunday alone, not related to
> ticketing. We normally would have 10,000 hits a day – 80,000! The
> volume is amazing. Apparently there are bulletin boards going out in
> China saying ... attack the MIFF website. (quoted in Metherell, 2009)

The exemption of films from classification for festival and community screenings is a common practice. The section on 'How to get a theatrical work classified' on the British Board of Film Classification (BBFC) website states: 'All feature films, short films and trailers which are shown theatrically must be classified by the BBFC, unless permission has been granted by the local authority in the area that the work is being shown.' This is an entirely different approach to the centralized process in Australia, as the authority to screen without a BBFC classification is handled by local licensing authorities. Although in practice it is very rare, in terms of theatrical distribution, the final word still remains with local licensing authorities, which are free, under the 2003 Licensing Act, to ignore the BBFC classification (BBFC website). An interesting case involves the London FrightFest and its scheduling of the now notorious *A Serbian Film* (2010) on 29 August 2010. At this time, the film had also been submitted to the BBFC for DVD and Blu-ray release, but it had not yet been classified. In this particular case, the local licensing authority was Westminster, with whom the festival had a 'special agreement' that allowed them to screen films that had not been classified by the BBFC to an adult audience. When rumours began circulating about the 'film's extreme content' and Westminster Council began receiving complaints about the proposed screening, it 'took the unusual step of directing that the film could only be screened at the festival if it had been classified by the BBFC' (SBBFC, 2011). Under pressure for a swift response, the BBFC examined the controversial film and, due predominantly to scenes of 'sexual and sexualised violence and scenes juxtaposing images of sex and sexual violence with images of children', they requested a total of '49 individual cuts ... across 11 scenes' (SBBFC, 2011). In an interview with *Screendaily*, FrightFest co-director Alan Jones explained why the festival decided not to go ahead with the screening of a heavily cut version;

'as a festival with a global integrity, we think a film of this nature should be shown in entirety as per the director's intention' (quoted in Wiseman, 2010).

As previously mentioned, unlike Australia and the UK, the US has adopted a voluntary approach to classification and rating. However, the MPAA members, the six major motion picture studios: Walt Disney, Paramount, Sony, Twentieth Century-Fox, Universal and Warner Bros., have all agreed that theatrically released films should be classified and rated by the Classification and Rating Administration (CARA), an entity established by the MPAA and the National Association of Theatre Owners, Inc. (NATO). CARA's 'Classification and Rating Rules' document states under 'Article 11 Submission of Motion Pictures for Rating':

> G. Any motion picture not produced or theatrically distributed by a member of the MPAA may be submitted to CARA for rating in the same manner and under the same conditions as those applicable to submission of motion pictures by members of the MPAA. However, the producer or distributor of such a motion picture may elect not to accept the rating and rating descriptor for that motion picture, or to surrender the rating for the motion picture, and therefore may exhibit or distribute the motion picture in the United States without a rating.

As with Australia and the UK, films screened at film festivals and community events in the US require no classification. Controversy can therefore arise at these events, with pressure groups at times attempting to ensure the cancellation of screenings. The Sundance Film Festival has been a regular site of campaigning from pressure groups. Interestingly, these actions can affect the reception and distribution of films in very different ways, especially as Sundance now functions as a buyers' market, where public and media interest can help guarantee distribution or tarnish a film's reputation forever (Craig, 2004, pp. 152–3; de Valck, 2007, p. 102). Two divergent cases worth mentioning are the 2007 screening of *Hounddog*, by writer and director Deborah Kampmeier, and the scheduling of Kevin Smith's *Red State* in 2011.

*Hounddog* stars Dakota Fanning, who was twelve years' old at the time, but whose character in the film is only nine. Set in 1950s Alabama, the film is about a young girl who, despite a life of poverty and abuse, finds happiness in music, especially in the blues. The scene that outraged audiences and led to personal attacks on the star's family, and her mother in particular, was one of rape:

> The scene in question involves a boy in his late teens who lures Fanning's character to an abandoned shack with promises of Elvis Presley tickets. The scene lasts less than a minute, and no simulation of a sex act is depicted on camera. The viewer sees flashes of Dakota's face, hand and foot as she falls, but the camera looks away as she begins to cry. No nudity is shown, though all involved in the movie agree it is a disturbing sequence. (Breznican, 2007)

Both the co-star Robin Wright Penn and Deborah Kampmeier acknowledged that the screening had been preceded by months of criticism from people who had not seen the film. Some audience members at Sundance emerged outraged while family and religious groups protested that it was criminal to feature such a young actress in a rape scene (Breznican, 2007). The criminal complaint, however, did not gain traction, with law-enforcement agencies and officials in North Carolina clearing Kampmeier of accusations of child exploitation (Anonymous, 2008). Kampmeier, defending the film, insisted that no harm had been done to her young star and that no physical contact had even taken place:

> When you take a shot of Dakota coming in the door, her foot tripping, a boy moving towards the camera, her face saying 'stop,' and you put them together in the editing room you get a rape scene. We never rehearsed a rape scene. She never acted out a rape scene; it's all so technical. I was a foot away from her face when we were shooting her face, which is all we have, other than her hands, in the rape scene. I was

> a foot away saying, 'Hold your breath, hold your breath, don't make a sound. Hold it, hold it, don't make a sound.' And then we'd go into the editing room and we'd remove my voice saying that and have her do an additional dialog recording session. Why is it that people see heads blown off in movies all the time and no one says, 'Oh my God, did they really have their head blown off?' (quoted in Anonymous, 2008)

While the director continued to insist that she took the utmost care to protect her young star, the film struggled to find distribution and was banned by a leading US cinema chain (Anonymous, 2008). The screening at Sundance took place on 22 January 2007; the film eventually received an R rating and only gained a limited release on 19 September 2008. Reviewing the film for the *Village Voice*, Michelle Orange noted:

> Having lurched through a gauntlet of Sundance jeers, recuts, and release delays, writer/director Deborah Kampmeier's *Hounddog* – at least as far as the press notes indicate (urgently) – now exists as a version different from the one that met such derision. (2008)

Orange's statement draws attention to the way in which exemption laws around film festivals, community screenings and events can create a space outside the regular distribution patterns for films to be screened in their original form.

The notorious Westboro Baptist Church group was at the centre of the hullabaloo around Smith's *Red State*. Often labelled a hate organization, the independent Baptist group from Kansas is well known for its extreme anti-homosexual stance, the wielding of hate-signs and the picketing of military servicemen's funerals. After demonstrating at churches in Salt Lake City, the group moved on to the Sundance Film Festival in Park City to protest against Smith's film, which satirizes Christian fundamentalism and ultra-conservatism. This independent film set in middle America involves teenagers responding to online invitations for sex, which lead to encounters with a sinister, hate-filled preacher who murders people he believes to be gay. When the infamous group arrived in Park City, it was met by a counterprotest of local Park High School Seniors, who were joined by members of the public. The protest took on a humorous note when members of the Westboro group, who believe the film directly satirizes them, were confronted by the counterprotesters also carrying signs, the messages of which mostly consisted of nonsense (Clark, 2011). The *Daily Mail* reported:

> A group of five Westboro Baptist Church members held signs with such slogans as 'God hates America', 'You're going to hell' and 'God is not mocked'. One church member told the newspaper it was 'just a beautiful preaching opportunity'. The film fans, numbering about 100 mainly high school students, stood jeering just a few feet opposite them. The pro-film crowd carried their own picket signs that spelled out messages such as 'Shut up and dance' and 'God hates signs'. 'We think they are spewing nonsense so we're spewing nonsense right back at them,' one demonstrator said. (Anonymous, 2011)

Similar reports were carried across a broad range of newspapers, ensuring excellent international publicity for the film, which Smith originally claimed would be auctioned off at a post-festival screening event. Smith ultimately retained the distribution rights to *Red State* through his own production company, Smodcast Pictures (Anonymous, 2011).

## Distribution, Neglect and Controversy

In returning to a discussion of the controversial nature of *Bad Boy Bubby*, what we can say is that its festival screenings caused little disruption, but around the time it gained acceptance to the Venice Film Festival, Hope claims he heard that distributors were proving unforthcoming – all because of the cat. The perceived ill treatment of the cat occurs in the first part of the film while

Bubby is still a prisoner within his mother's flat. He occupies his time by dismembering cockroaches and inflicting indignities on a cat, many of these tortures similar to those regularly inflicted on him. While this sequence will be closely analyzed at a later point, for clarity's sake, controversy surrounded several scenes, which included: the cat with a cord tied around its neck being pulled by Bubby (see Figures 8 and 9); the same cat, dead, apparently having been suffocated in cling wrap (see Figure 12); and later in the film, the appearance of a dead kitten. Not surprisingly, some distributors and buyers found such treatment of an animal on screen offensive and were concerned about audience responses. On hearing this, Hope reports that the first assistant director, Paul Ammitzboll, retorted: 'They aren't concerned with your being raped in the film … or any of the abuse to you. Just with the cat. They're so hypocritical.' To which Hope replied 'Well I wasn't really being raped or abused … I was acting. The cat wasn't' (Hope, 2004, p. 35). *Bad Boy Bubby*'s initial success at the Venice Film Festival was soon overshadowed by attempts to have screenings of the film suspended.

After Venice, the film was released in a number of countries through various small art-house distributors, with varying degrees of success. Interest in the film ranged enormously, with de Heer claiming that in Norway it was the second highest grossing film of the year, running for twelve months, while it struggled to gain a foothold in America. Initially the film was bought for the US but a dispute arose over the contract; things went wrong; and, as de Heer suggests, 'a film gets old … past its use by date' (2010b). *Bad Boy Bubby* did have a minor US release in a few places, but the film seems to have passed the country by, with the director claiming that instead it developed a cult or underground following thanks to 'pirate copies' (2010b). Blue Underground eventually gave the film a limited video release on 26 April 2005, more than ten years after its completion. Concerns about animal cruelty never seem to have arisen and here we need to consider the different legal issues and public perceptions of animal-rights issues. For example, tail-docking and the pinning of dogs' ears has been banned in Australia since 2004; in England and Wales it has been restricted since 2006 and can only be undertaken by a vet on a number of working-dog breeds. In the US, however, such practices are entirely unrestricted (CBD website; BVA website).

In Australia the film was classified on 23 February 1994 with an R rating and the consumer advice, 'Adult themes; High level coarse language; Sex Scenes' (Australian Government Classification website). After the film's success at Venice and with the broader international film community, the distributor Village Roadshow picked up the Australian distribution rights for the film, and it was released nationally on 24 July 1994. While not censored in Australia, some reviewers treated the film with disdain and henceforth it developed more of a cult following. Its Australian box-office takings of AUD808,789 only just covered its production costs (Jameson, 1994, pp. 100–1).

The BBFC was the only classification board that requested changes to the film before its release. The BBFC website notes that when the film was classified for theatrical release on 19 October 1994, three seconds were cut to achieve an 18 rating, restricting it to an adult audience. While the rating is consistent across territories, this is the only incidence of the film being cut. J. L. Green, the chief assistant (policy) at the BBFC, outlined the cut and the reasons for it:

> Reel 1 – When Bubby maltreats the cat, remove section where he sits by kitchen table pulling the cat to him hard round its neck.
> This cut was replicated (at 8 1/2 minutes) when the work was classified for video in 1995. The cuts were made under the Cinematography Films (Animal) Act 1973.

With the cut made to the scene involving the cat, Entertainment Film Distribution released *Bad Boy Bubby* in the UK on 1 September 1994, and the video arm of the same company released a VHS version on 3 March 1995. When the work was resubmitted for video classification in 2007, J. L. Green commented on the decision to reinstate the material which was considered afresh and carefully re-examined. Under the Animals Act, the BBFC is obliged to consider scenes that 'involve the cruel infliction of pain and terror on an animal or the cruel goading of an animal to fury'. On this re-examination, it was judged that, while the cat may have experienced some discomfort, the action of pulling it by the cord did not constitute a cruel infliction of pain or goading. It was felt that the scene was neither severe nor protracted enough to qualify as 'cruel', the legal test. The distributor also presented detailed letters of assurance – one from the film's director – about the treatment and well-being of the cats on set. The letters noted that the Animal Welfare League of South Australia had been consulted about different aspects of the filming with the cats and that the film-makers complied with the principles laid out in the International Code for use of all animals in films by the World Society for the Protection of Animals. These letters had not been presented to the BBFC at the film's initial submission in the UK for film and video release, although submitted to film regulatory bodies in other countries. Taking all these factors into consideration, it was decided that the cut could be waived (2011) and Eureka Entertainment finally released the uncut version of the film on DVD in 2007 (BBFC).

## The Italian Contradiction

The UK, however, was not the only place the film was to prove controversial. A little more than a year after *Bad Boy Bubby*'s extraordinary Venetian success, the film found itself in hot water after it was claimed that a cat had been tortured to death on screen. Overnight the film's award-winning reputation shifted and, instead of attracting plaudits, it became the target of attacks. The result was catastrophic for de Heer as the animal-cruelty claim coincided with his efforts to secure a worldwide release. He recalls how the statement about the cat's fate 'went into print, it became the truth and a coalition of seven different organizations largely working in animal rights planned an Italy wide boycott of all Australian products' (de Heer, 2010b). The story also appeared in a run of articles in Australian newspapers. The *Sydney Morning Herald* asserted that the film had 'come under the critical eye of Venice's magistrates after a complaint to the President of Italy, Mr. Oscar Luigi Scalfaro, regarding a scene in which a cat is tortured to death' (1994, p. 17). A regional councillor of the Italian Green Party, Michele Boato, requested that the President suspend all screenings of *Bad Boy Bubby* due to the alleged on-screen torture and suffocation of the cat. Another local newspaper, the *Age*, also picked up the story, with Desmond O'Grady reporting that an Italian magistrate was 'conducting an inquiry into the alleged torture and killing of a cat' after protests had been made against the film by 'environmentalists, animal welfare organisations' and the politician Boato (1994, p. 20). The article notes that, ironically, while the film had won five awards at the Venice Film Festival, it was in Venice that most of the protests were occurring. O'Grady quotes the film's producer, Procacci, who notes that before the film's commercial release in Italy, he 'sent the Italian Society for the Prevention of Cruelty to Animals a letter from Mr. Rolf de Heer', explaining that no animals had been tortured or killed during the film shoot. Procacci commented: 'What you see on the screen is one thing …. What happened during the film was something else' (quoted in O'Grady, 1994, p. 20). On another note, the producer also states that he was satisfied with the film's reception, which included 'good press', but only a 'so-so' response from audiences.

Discussion of the controversy can also be found on the Australian Screen website where in his 'Curator's Notes', Paul Byrnes (1993) ponders the issue of why the most controversial aspect of the film was not its depiction of cruelty towards humans, but the depiction of cruelty towards a cat:

> When the film was released in Italy, a collation of animal rights groups tried to set up a boycott of Australian products, alleging that the cat was tortured and smothered in the film. Rolf de Heer has said that none of that is true; the cat scenes were carefully filmed, with a veterinarian and animal cruelty inspector on set. Nicholas Hope, in an on-stage interview included on the DVD of the film, says there were two cats, one of which became the pet of a crew member. The other was a feral cat

that was put down by a vet after filming (as with most feral cats that are caught in Australia).

In Part 3, I discuss the treatment of cats on set during the making of the film, but the obvious response to Byrnes's ponderings is that the cruelty depicted against Bubby in the film was represented, whereas the suspicion was that the cruelty against the cat was both actual and representational.

The Italian controversy seemed to quickly dissipate with no real action against the film or Australian imports, but it did cause some difficulties for the director with the Australian government. De Heer says the 'Australian Government came down heavily on me asking, "What the hell's going on here?"' But de Heer is adamant that the cat scenes were all carefully orchestrated, with a vet and animal-welfare people on set, and that one cat was even saved from death as it was adopted by one of the cast. Commenting on the feral-cat eradication programme, which continues in Australia today, the director says that the Animal Welfare League of South Australia supplied a feral cat which turned out not to be feral but a domestic stray – it was just 'scared and wanted to be loved'. It used to follow one of the cast around, was eventually adopted and lived another ten years. De Heer's sensibilities are clear, however, when he states, 'Look, I'm sorry but the degree of suffering felt by that feral cat for that one moment in the film is so infinitesimal compared to the real issues that beset the world today' (2010b).

Yet it is the issue of animal cruelty that sparked the most controversy around this film, and it is still a focus of concern for animal-rights groups even today. As noted in the introduction to this volume, *Bad Boy Bubby* continues to be the subject of grassroots activism, with the film listed as one to boycott by animal-rights groups, online communities and individual bloggers. Again, in relation to this debate, it is important to note that, while discussions of censorship generally relate to perceptions of the possible harm done to an audience through the experience of watching a film, animal cruelty is a legal issue to do with the harmful treatment of an animal on set during production. To further illuminate the relations between animal-rights laws, film censorship and social sentiments to do with the treatment of animals, the next section will discuss these issues, examining the UK Cinematograph Films (Animals) 1937 Act and the later Animal Welfare Act of 2006. A brief history of the Australian government's feral-cat eradication programme will also be outlined, before I undertake a close analysis of the scenes in *Bad Boy Bubby* involving the cat – or, more accurately, the cats.

# ✖ Part 3

## ANIMAL CRUELTY AND THE CINEMA

I still remember when I first saw Thomas Edison's *Electrocuting an Elephant* (1903) as a student. It left me speechless – this huge 'beast' enslaved – one moment alive and the next dead. I hoped its 'murder' was some clever circus trick but I somehow knew by the way the elephant fell, the speed with which it happened and the puffs of smoke (I guessed the exudes caused by burnt hide that escaped from the contraptions and electrodes that imprisoned its feet) that it was truly dead. After collapsing, the elephant quivers momentarily and is then still, as if confirming its expiration. I have not been able to bring myself to watch this film again and it was only in more recent years that I discovered more about the film – and its elephant. Topsy was a mankiller. Originally owned by the Forepaugh Circus, she spent her final years at Coney Island's Luna Park. She was a 'park' animal that had killed three men, one of whom was her trainer, who found it amusing to feed her lit cigarettes. An exotic circus animal is a costly item, but her 'murderous' actions meant she was deemed disposable. Then enter the scene Thomas Edison, inventor and businessman, whose history reveals a legacy of killing animals through electrocution, the incentive being to 'sabotage the development of AC (alternating current) electrical generators, which delivered electricity at a higher voltage and to greater distances than his own DC (direct current) systems' (Lippit, 2002). Edison's intent was to discredit his primary competition and its major proponent, the Westinghouse Electrical and Manufacturing Company. Topsy's electrocution was captured on film at Coney Island on 4 January 1903, in front of a crowd of approximately 1,500 spectators. She was fed poison-laced carrots first to subdue her and Edison's one-minute single-reel actuality captured the event for posterity (Lippit, 2002). Lisa Cartwright makes the astute observation that the sequence 'suggests not so much the destruction of an animal as the execution of a criminal' (quoted in Lippit, 2002), while the name Topsy – a toy, a plaything kind of a name – informs a gradual anthropomorphosis of the elephant.

## Animal Cruelty and Audience Affect

Having experienced a powerful response to seeing the documentary footage of an elephant being electrocuted for some kind of experiment, I am acutely aware of the way in which acts of animal cruelty can affect an audience. Over the years I have taught many classes on documentary and on-screen violence. Yet, without fail, I am constantly surprised by the way in which students respond to perceived cruelty to animals on film, be it dramatized or real. Allakariallak, the Inuit who played the central protagonist of Robert Flaherty's *Nanook of the North* (1922), died of starvation several years after the film's completion, having travelled deeper into the Canadian Arctic in search of food. While we all know that many of the scenes in this film were re-enactments, the knowledge of the harshness of these people's living conditions seems to have little effect on the dismay and horror that students express about the 'primitive' killing of seals and walruses for food. On questioning students, I find their responses consistent; while they understand and respect Nanook's need to kill for survival, they consider animals like children – innocent and in need of protection. The history of the cinema, however, bears powerful witness to their continued mistreatment in both fiction and non-fiction film.

Many of us are appalled by the killing and torture of animals, their restrictive confinement or their cruel slaughter. The last decade in Australia has seen vigorous lobbying to ban the transport of Australian sheep to the Middle East as unnecessary and inhumane (CIWF website, 2010). In June 2011, public outrage over footage on the *Four Corners* (1961–) investigative television show revealing the appalling treatment of Australian cattle in eleven Indonesian abattoirs resulted in the government swiftly placing a ban on all live exports of cattle to Indonesia (Worthington, 2011). However, the public revulsion over the abattoirs' footage and my own students' dismay at perceived animal cruelty on film do not necessarily correspond with actions to eliminate cruelty to animals in society. This is partly because animal cruelty encompasses more than just extreme cases such as this, evidenced in the footage of the Australian cattle being brutalized before slaughter, with the RSPCA claiming that some of the animals appeared to be still alive while being dismembered (Worthington, 2011). Cruelty is frequently about the neglect of an animal and the failure to report or act on it (Brown, 1988). In the case of the cinema, we will happily watch a protagonist being killed or tortured but scenes of animal cruelty, or even mercy killings where the family pet needs to be euthanized, seem to trigger all our emotional registers, which in the cinema are already primed and open to empathy. We are unfettered from the actualities of our social existence – of our tendency to not want to be involved, of our lack of time, of our resolve to mind our own business.

In more recent times, the issues of animal rights and animal treatment have come to the foreground. In *The Animals Reader: The Essential Classic and Contemporary Writings*, Linda Kalof and Amy Fitzgerald outline how, since the 1970s, the 'animal question' has undergone a 'sweeping reevaluation':

> It is now widely acknowledged that, in addition to human-driven habitat loss and species extinction, untold numbers of animals are commodified for consumption, exhibition, labor, science and recreation, only to be discarded when they have outlived their usefulness – when indeed they are allowed to live at all. In addition, many now recognize the pernicious link between our relationship with other animals and some of the most pernicious human social problems, such as slavery, sexism and environmental degradation. (2007, p. xiv)

The link between animals and humans has further ramifications in relation to beliefs about the escalation of aberrant human behaviour. There is also a commonly held belief that animal cruelty practised by children can evolve into more serious aberrant behaviours in later life. Since the psychiatrist J. M. Macdonald published his pioneering study in 1963, animal cruelty has been viewed as one of three predictive indicators of a broad range of disorder behaviours. These behaviours, the Macdonald Triad, which is also known as the triad of sociopathy, are 'bedwetting (enuresis), fire setting and torturing small animals' (Merz-Perez and Heide, 2004, p. 6). However, as Randall Lockwood writes in his foreword to Linda Merz-Perez and Kathleen Heide's *Animal Cruelty: Pathway to Violence against People*: 'One of the greatest challenges to those of us concerned about crime and violence is that there are so many potential forces at work that can lead an individual down many, many different paths' (2004, p. 3). Referring us back to the cinema, Lockwood comments that almost every American born in the twentieth century

> learned a lesson in connections between animal abuse and human violence when, in the film *The Wizard of Oz*, they heard the Wicked Witch of the West threaten Dorothy and Toto with, 'I'll get you … and your little dog too.' (2004, p. xi)

Yet attempts to confirm the widely held belief in this connection have generally failed, partly because many children and young adults who torture animals were themselves the victims of abuse. But this is not to say that abused children always grow up to be abusive adults, even though a history of torturing pets and small animals has, historically, served as a diagnostic criterion for conduct disorders from antisocial behaviours through to known psychopathologies. Significantly, many of us, particularly as children, have at some point in our lives treated an animal or small pet in an uncaring way – or, more commonly, we have participated in cruelty through neglect or failing to prevent an animal's mistreatment.

As the above discussion would suggest, feelings about animal cruelty come with a certain cultural bias so it is not surprising that the treatment of the cat in *Bad Boy Bubby* generated widely divergent responses. To gain a better understanding of why the film became controversial in some territories and not others, I will examine the different laws that regulate the treatment of animals in the UK and US, and across Australia, specifically in relation to the cinema before moving on in the next section to a close analysis of the controversial sequences.

## Laws and Regulations

As the UK was the only territory to cut *Bad Boy Bubby* before release, I will address this legislation first. As previously mentioned, animal cruelty is a legal issue and the laws of a particular country generally inform censorship in this regard. The BBFC lists two important Acts that cover animal welfare and that have to be taken into consideration when classifying work. The earliest is the Cinematograph Films (Animals) Act 1937 which 'prohibits the exhibition or distribution' of films 'in connection with the production of which suffering may have been caused to animals; and for purposes connected therewith' (Legislation.gov.uk website). The Act primarily prohibits the exhibition of films that involve the 'cruel infliction of pain or terror on any animal or the cruel goading of any animal to fury'. (The statement resonates with J. L. Green's comments about why *Bad Boy Bubby* was initially cut due to perceived acts of cruelty.) The second is the 2006 Animal Welfare Act. This more recent legislation also makes it 'illegal to show or publish a recording of an animal fight which has taken place within Great Britain since 6 April 2007' (BBFC website, undated).

While the first Act did not become law until 1937, it was informed by the original Cruelty to Animals Act of 1876, which was initially passed by parliament to regulate experimentation on animals. In fact, the UK has a significant history of animal-rights activism. In the nineteenth century, a period in which animals were thought of as objects of utility – 'beasts of burden' – only useful for work, sport or food, the Society for the Prevention of Cruelty to Animals was launched in London in 1824. It was the first national animal-protection society in the world (RSPCA website), which with Queen Victoria's permission became the Royal Society for the Prevention of Cruelty to Animals in 1840.

In the early years of the cinema in both the UK and US, the animal-cruelty problem centred around the treatment of horses, especially when tripwires were engaged to cause falls, collapses and somersaults, often resulting in broken limbs and sometimes death or the need to euthanize an injured animal. During the late 1930s and earlier 1940s the RSPCA began to monitor the use of such devices and by the 1950s the training of horses for stuntwork became a more common practice. Even in the contemporary era, we can still clearly see the effects of the first Act with regard to horses in films, particularly with the video release of American films in the UK.[5] Films that have been cut in recent times include *The Legend of the Lone Ranger* (1981); released on video in 2000 in the UK, it had five seconds cut, of which the BBFC website notes: 'Cuts required to two shots of horses suffering harm while falling in accordance with Cinematograph Films (Animals) Act 1937'. In the same year, *Rambo III* (1988) was released on video and was cut by two seconds due to the 'sight of illegal horse fall', in accordance with the same Act. Another well-known case involving horses concerned Warren Beatty's *Reds* (1981), which had eight seconds cut for video release: 'Cuts were required to genuine animal cruelty (in this case the cruel tripping of three horses during a battle in line with the BBFC Guidelines and Policy.' Other examples of films cut for this reason include the extremely controversial Italian production *Cannibal Holocaust* (1980), which had nearly six minutes cut from the video release to 'scenes involving real cruelty to animals and to eroticised sexual violence, in accordance with BBFC policy and guidelines'. The South Korean film *The Isle* (2003), directed by Kim Ki-Duk, had one minute and fifty seconds of cuts that included 'four compulsory cuts ... to the sight of animal cruelty in accordance with the Cinematograph Films (Animals) Act 1937' (BBFC website).

*The Times* published in its editorial a response from American James Ferman, the director of the BBFC from 1975 to 1999, to a letter suggesting that the BBFC allowed images of horses tripped with wires. The letter referred to a debate that Ferman had participated in at a public meeting in Birmingham. He responded:

> Citing the 1937 Act of Parliament which makes it illegal to show any scene in the making of which an animal was treated cruelly, I showed some examples commenting that horses can't be trained to do

> somersaults, and many have been killed just to make an exciting
> sequence. In films, the only snuff sequences we see at the board are
> those that involve the slaughter of animals. We see them, but you don't
> because we cut them out, as the law requires, before the films are
> released. The BBFC is the strictest authority in the world on cruelty to
> animals in films, regularly consulting the RSPCA and the American
> Humane Association when the issue is in doubt. We are backed by an
> exceptionally humane example of British law, which enables us to ban
> cockfights, animal baiting and torture of the most distressing kinds. Our
> rigorous enforcement of this law will continue. (1998, p. 21)

We can take Ferman at his word when he claims that the UK has some of the most humane laws in the world. The laws have also been enforced retrospectively or have been called upon when controversy has arisen. The more recent Animal Welfare Act, which deals specifically with animal fights, was invoked in an interesting way with regard to the Edinburgh Film Festival screening in 1974 and a more recent screening at the National Film Theatre in 1985 of Monte Hellman's *Cockfighter* (1974). Set in the American deep south and shot on a shoestring budget, the film is considered a cult classic by many critics, specifically due to Warren Oates's extraordinary performance as the silent brooding cock trainer, but the film is also notorious for its real live cockfights. *Cockfighter* was due to be revived at the 2006 Edinburgh Film Festival; however, the screening was cancelled after the organizers learned that the film violates both Acts due to its recording of cockfights. Significantly, the previous screenings were actually illegal and the film is no longer available in the UK, as it has never been classified, although it can be 'bought on DVD abroad and imported' (Hoyle, 2006, p. E.5). One can assume that, due to film festival regulations, the film required no classification for its original screening at the Edinburgh Film Festival.

Another example of a recent British film that has come to the attention of humane societies is Guy Ritchie's *Snatch* (2000), in which it is alleged that several hares were torn to pieces by dogs. These days it is usual for humane societies and RSPCA members to monitor productions involving animals. This was not the case with Ritchie's film and, once the RSPCA heard allegations about the film's supposed mistreatment of animals, the society asked to see footage. The film-makers denied the allegations that animals were mistreated, and the film version that audiences now see shows all the hares escaping (Anonymous, 2000, p. A2). First-time Mexican director Gonzales Inarritu also found his film *Amores Perros* (2000) under the spotlight. While the film won numerous awards around the world, the dog-fighting scenes brought the film to the BBFC's attention. Despite the film's success at the Edinburgh and London Film Festivals, it struggled to find a UK distributor due to the controversy. While Inarritu argues that no animal was harmed and the action all lies in the editing, the twenty-one seconds of footage that revolve around an illegal dog-fighting den in Mexico City put the board in a difficult situation. At the time, Sue Clarke of the BBFC commented:

> We are looking at the film very carefully. Our only problem is with one short scene and the reason we are taking so long to decide is that we can see its importance to the film. Let's be very clear, it is not the board that is the obstacle here, it is the law, and the law says animals should not be goaded or in any way incited to fight. (quoted in Gibbons, 2001, p. 5)

The film was eventually released uncut.

It is the American Humane Association (AHA) that has been most influential in attempting to ensure the benevolent treatment of animals on film and television sets in America. The association developed out of the humane movement of the 1860s and made important inroads into American culture during the Civil War. However, it was during the 1950s that the Nobel Peace prize-winner Albert Schweitzer's philosophies and his 'reverence for life' concept led to the consolidation of the movement (Humane Society of the United States website). Yet the power of the AHA is not tied into the laws guiding censorship, as it is in the UK. In *Animal Law: Cases and Materials*

(2006), Sonia Waisman *et al.* claim that since the 1980s, anxiety about the use and treatment of animals in audiovisual works has grown. They suggest that, while there is a great 'concern by animal advocates' about pre-production training behind closed doors, 'the conditions on the set, in many instances, are far from idyllic' (2006, p. 445). They also comment that there is little case law addressing the treatment of animals in these contexts:

> Since the 1980s, a clause in the Screen Actors Guild ('SAG') contract with producers has granted sole authority for monitoring the treatment of animals in movies, television shows, commercials and music videos to the Film and Television Unit of the American Humane Association. ... Although the contract covers 'most significant productions in the U.S.' ... interviews and internal documents revealed that ... the Unit 'lacks any meaningful enforcement power under the SAG contract, depends on major studios to pay for its operations and is rife with conflicts of interest'. (Waisman *et al.*, 2006, p. 445)

The end-credit disclaimer on films that we are all so familiar with, 'No animals were harmed', offers the audience the assurance that the AHA has been doing its job on sets using trained or wild animals. However, as the 'Guidelines for the Safe Use of Animals in Filmed Media' states in bold:

> **Production is responsible for contacting the American Humane when animals are to be used. It is not the responsibility of the trainer/ wrangler/supplier to do so. Only the American Humane's on-set supervision can qualify a production for official end-credit disclaimer eligibility.** (1994–2009, p. 5)

Therefore, whereas the UK has specifically legislated against animal cruelty in films, with guidelines guaranteeing humane treatment, safeguarding animals in the US industry depends on productions voluntarily submitting to outside supervision. On some level, the cooperation of the film-makers relies on the viewing public determining to see only films endorsed by the AHA. Yet, while the system is less regulated, many humane societies and animal-rights groups make it their business to attempt to ensure the protection of animals used in media. One of the pivotal films discussed in relation to US regulations is Michael Cimino's *Heaven's Gate* (1980), a bleak Western based in Montana during the late 1800s. The film's treatment of animals caused worldwide controversy and it was cut in the UK; the animal action involves actual cockfights, several horse trips and a horse being blown up with a rider on its back. The owner of a horse that was abused on set filed a lawsuit against the producers, director and horse wrangler. The AHA review of the film states:

> The case was settled out of court. AHA, which was barred from monitoring the animal action on the set, protested the film by distributing an international press release detailing the animal cruelty in *Heaven's Gate* and asking people to boycott the film ... . The controversy surrounding the animal action in *Heaven's Gate* prompted the Screen Actors Guild (SAG) and the Alliance of Motion Picture & Television Producers (AMPTP) to contractually authorize AHA oversight of animals in filmed media. (American Humane Association website)

The controversy precipitated a change in the working practices of US film and media industries. The SAG website now states:

> The Producer-Screen Actors Codified Basic agreement must notify the American Humane Association prior to the commencement of any work that involves animals. This section also provides representation of the American Humane Association with access to sets while animals are being used. (Russell, 1997)

We can begin to see, however, that unlike in the UK, the US system is open to abuse, with the producer the sole figure responsible for ensuring the AHA is on set whenever animals are involved. Only SAG members are governed by these legal requirements regarding the treatment of animals. This is not to say that controversies might not arise or legal action be taken against specific films, but it happens on an individual basis. However, most of the MPAA see an AHA stamp of approval as an important part of a film's appeal to the populace, who are generally offended by animal cruelty. More recently, CGI has enabled various acts to be depicted digitally with barely a real animal in sight. Douglas Martin suggests that, while animal abuse is a felony and films like *Babe* (1995) have produced representations of animals that the most 'ardent animal-rights activists applaud', the 'CGI bashing of animals' has become an international 'laugh-getter' in film, television and advertising:

> In the film 'There's Something about Mary,' a small dog flies out a window. In 'As Good as it Gets,' a pooch is crammed down a trash chute. In 'EdTV', a love scene culminates in Matthew McConaughey falling on a cat. In 'Men in Black,' an alien-pug confesses after it is mercilessly shaken. Even the preview for 'Idle Hands' shows a cat being swung around by its tail. (1999, p. 4)

In conclusion, Martin suggests that the jury is still out on whether the 'CGI' animal abuse is simply harmless entertainment or something much more disturbing. Referring back to my earlier discussion of the continuum between children who abuse animals and who then present antisocial behaviours as young adults, this could be an area that warrants further investigation.

## The Peculiar Case of 'Crush Videos'

With no clear consensus between the AHA and US laws to protect animals, some unusual irregularities occur in the implementation of these regulations. While dogfights and animal cruelty have long been illegal in all states, a 1999 Federal law that banned trafficking in 'depictions of animal cruelty' was struck down in the Supreme Court in 2010. Adam Liptak notes in his article

'Justices Reject Ban on Videos of Animal Cruelty' that the ban does not relate to the actual activity – cruelty to animals – but rather to 'trafficking' in the recordings of 'conduct in which a living animal is intentionally maimed, mutilated, tortured, wounded or killed' (2010). When Bill Clinton originally signed the Bill, prompted by the First Amendment, he acknowledged reservations and requested the Justice Department to 'limit prosecutions to "wanton cruelty to animals designed to appeal to prurient interest in sex"'. Clinton was specifically referring to so-called 'crush videos' that feature (generally) women slowly crushing animals (usually kittens) to death while wearing high-heeled spike shoes or sometimes in bare feet, all the while talking to the animal in a kind of 'dominatrix patter' as it squeals in agony (Liptak, 2010). Significantly, the legislation effectively quashed the abhorrent 'crush-video' industry. Liptak's article and another by Stanley Fish, entitled 'The First Amendment and Kittens' published in the *New York Times* in April 2010, were written in response to Chief Justice John Roberts's announcement that the Supreme Court had struck down the statute 'criminalizing the production and sale of videos depicting animal cruelty in a manner intended to satisfy a particular "sexual fetish"' (Fish, 2010). The Supreme Court felt that the law restricted individual First Amendment rights to freedom of speech, its parameters so broad that it could have an impact on legal activities such as the video recording of hunting or selling magazines about that pursuit. The law was to be rewritten to deal specifically with crush videos and other depictions of animal cruelty (Fish, 2010). The House of Representatives and the Senate passed Bill H.R. 5566, which prohibits interstate commerce in animal crush videos on 28 November 2010 and President Obama signed it on 9 December 2010 (Govtrack.us website).

## Australia and Animal Rights

The 'sweeping reevaluation' of the 'animal question' that Kalof and Fitzgerald (2007) saw as beginning in the 1970s was slow to make its presence felt in

Australia. It was 2001 before the two main bodies governing animal welfare, the Department of Primary Industries and the RSPCA Australia both completed reviews. The Department of Primary Industries website, which lists the 'Code of Practice for the Welfare of Film Animals', released its reviewed legislation in October of that year. The department states that, in relation to legislation regarding the treatment of animals, it is important to refer to state practices due to variations in laws:

> State and territory legislation generally makes it an offence to be cruel to animals. The Prevention of Cruelty to Animals Act (NSW 1979) is typical; making it a criminal offence to commit acts of cruelty or aggravated cruelty (as defined, but including killing) to any animal or to be a party to such offences.
>
> Companies and persons using animals in film and television productions are advised to familiarise themselves with the relevant act in each state and territory.

The 'Code of Practice for the Welfare of Film Animals' lists the general requirements to ensure the well-being of a trained, domestic or wild animal in a film or on a television set in Australia. The guidelines are very similar to those in both the US and the UK: all animals are to be maintained in a clean environment, watered and well fed, and not placed under stress; horse 'falls should not be achieved by trip-wires or pitfalls' (Department of Primary Industries website). But there are some surprises that would provoke the ire of many an animal activist, including a couple of points pertinent to *Bad Boy Bubby*:

- A qualified veterinarian is the only person able to prescribe drugs, including tranquillisers. S/he should examine all animals prior to use to ensure their good health and that they have received all appropriate inoculations and medication. Some animals such as reptiles should not be sedated … .

- Sedation or tranquillisation of animals to alter behaviour or performance may only occur if supervised by a veterinarian and after discussion has made it clear that the same effect cannot be achieved with a fake or trained animal. Undue pressure for heavy or lengthy sedation of animals should not be placed on veterinarians … .
- A receipt of purchase should be held by the production office for any dead animals acquired for use in scenes. Such animals should not have been killed expressly for the production … .

As will be discussed in depth in the next section, de Heer and his crew claim a veterinarian was on set to sedate one of the cats for a short period of time and the Animal Welfare League of South Australia, which collects stray and feral cats and, in some cases, euthanizes them, supplied the crew with a dead cat for one scene. I imagine for many people, however, the sedation of an animal for the sake of a scene would be viewed as a kind of cruelty – playing with the animal's health and possibly its life. It is obviously not something we would ever consider doing to a human being. Yet the guidelines would seem to support de Heer and his production's claims that no animal was harmed during the making of *Bad Boy Bubby*. Their treatment of cats on set seemed to adhere to the legislation.

The Australian Classification Guidelines refer directly to the RSPCA as the authority on the treatment of animals. The 2001 'Review of the Classification Guidelines for Films and Computer Games' states under its listing on animals:

> The RSPCA Australia submitted that the Guidelines 'must reflect current community attitudes towards animal welfare, the treatment of animals and broad community abhorrence to cruelty being done to animals'. In particular, the RSPCA recommended that 'a film be refused classification if it contains the actual killing or injuring of an animal'.
> (Brand, 2001, p. 47)

The legal requirements regarding animals are now highly regulated, but this was not the case when *Bad Boy Bubby* was released. While the Australian government was upset by the controversy de Heer's film caused in Venice; on *Bad Boy Bubby*'s first release in Australia it was granted an R rating, with no mention of animal cruelty. A few years after the film's release, the states began to pass more rigorous legislation to cover the treatment of animals in film productions. In 1997, Lynden Barber noted in the *Australian* newspaper that: 'All filmmakers will be required to notify the NSW [New South Wales] RSPCA or Animal Welfare League before an animal can be used in the State's film, television and stage productions.' Barber cited the 'use of a dead cat in *Bad Boy Bubby* and the killing of an injured horse without a veterinary surgeon present in *The Man from Snowy River* as cases that must be outlawed' (p. 10).

*Bad Boy Bubby* was again mentioned in a public debate in 1998, which accompanied screenings of Harmony Korine's *Gummo* (1997) at the Melbourne International Film Festival. At the time *Gummo* was beset by worldwide controversy, with animal-rights groups protesting against its screening due to its depiction of brutal acts of animal and human cruelty. Animal Liberation Victoria picketed outside the Melbourne Film Festival screening on 9 August 1998 with spokeswoman Rheya Linden stating: 'I'm very upset at how cats are treated in this film … There is a lot of prejudice towards cats in the community and I think filmmakers need to be careful depicting cruelty to cats' (Zwar, 1998, p. 19). To gain a better understanding of the prejudice towards cats in Australian society, we need to consider the 'stray-' and 'feral-cat' issue and eradication policies still in place across Australia.

## Domestic, Feral or Stray?

While cats are popular pets in Australia, along with dogs, most local governments impose strict curfews governing when domestic cats can roam outside and when they must be contained in a cat enclosure or the family home. Generally, cats must be contained from sunset to sunrise due to the destruction they wreak on Australia's distinct native birds and animals through nocturnal hunting. While responsible pet owners can greatly reduce the damage caused by their cats through abiding by the curfew restrictions and neutering their pets, it is stray and specifically feral cats that cause most of the problems. As the Humane Society (of the US) notes, while a stray cat is a lost or abandoned pet, a feral cat is either the offspring of stray or feral cats. While strays are accustomed to human contact, feral cats are wild: they do not adapt easily to living with humans and they cause the most damage to native fauna. The Department of the Environment, Water, Heritage and the Arts notes:

> The first recorded instance of cats being brought to Australia was by English settlers in the 18th century, although cats may have arrived much earlier with other human visitors (Baldwin 1980). Cats were deliberately released into the wild during the 19th century to control rabbits and mice (Rolls 1969). Today there are about 18 million feral cats in Australia (McLeod 2004), distributed through all habitats (except some of the wettest rainforests) in mainland Australia and Tasmania and on many offshore islands.
>
> Feral cats are a serious vertebrate pest in Australia, and have severe effects on native fauna. (Threat Abatement Plan for Predation by Feral Cats, 2008)

With hindsight, we look back on the introduction of cats to control other devastating introduced 'pests' – rabbits and mice – as a kind of madness, which also included the introduction of the fox, in this case, for sport, and so on. In 1995, the Australian government's Department of Sustainability, Environment, Water, Population and Communities published an overview of the threat caused by feral cats. In 1999, it released its 'threat abatement plan' for predation by feral cats that was replaced in 2001 by a reviewed threat abatement plan (TAP), which 'establishes a national framework to guide and coordinate Australia's response to the impacts of feral cats on biodiversity' ('The Feral Cat (*Felis Catus*)', 2001). The document makes for bleak reading, outlining the decimation and loss of many native birds and animals due to introduced species such as cats. The notion that feral cats could actually be eradicated by a range of measures including traps, poison and sterilization has, in more recent times, given way to attempts to contain their numbers and to prevent them occupying new areas, with eradication only attempted on 'high-conservation-value "islands"'.

The Australian Classification Board's failure to respond to the treatment of cats in *Bad Boy Bubby* is indicative of the fact that animal-rights campaigners were slow to make an impact in Australia. Furthermore, media awareness, lobbying and advertising has ensured that at a time when Australian society is becoming more and more environmentally aware, the feral cat is perceived as a serious danger to native fauna. Although legislation concerning the treatment of animals is now more rigorous, there is some ambivalence – and possibly still a level of prejudice – when it comes to cats, specifically feral cats. If we think back to the 1970s and take for example a film such as the Australian co-production *Wake in Fright* (1971), we can, however, see a radical change in the last fifty years regarding public perceptions of animal cruelty in film. Today, audiences are generally appalled by the footage of a real 'kangaroo shoot' in *Wake in Fright*. While a trained kangaroo was used in some scenes, a disclaimer at the end of the film states that the images of the hunting and killing of kangaroos were part of a required organized cull. While this is true, the footage of animals in flight, collapsing as they are hit by bullets, freezing in the glare of headlights, bounding away in fright from high-powered vehicles tracking their paths and the close-up images of slowly dying beasts, particularly where there has not been a clean kill, are gut-wrenching to watch. The hunt was legal at the time, but the recorded action appears to have been dramatized for the cameras. While there are still occasional kangaroo culls, footage like this would never be allowed to make its way into a fiction film, although it could become part of the body of a documentary or news report. These days, Australian audiences are much more sensitive to the treatment of animals, especially of one of their national symbols. In turning to a consideration of animal cruelty in *Bad Boy Bubby*, it is helpful to keep in mind issues such as the context of the period, changes to legislation about the treatment of animals and the differences between domestic, stray and feral cats.

Animal cruelty is central to the notoriety of *Bad Boy Bubby*, yet it is apparent from the above discussion that there is still disparity between nations as to the degree of influence governments and regulatory bodies should be able to exercise on the treatment of animals in the media. While the UK has been a leader in legislating for animal rights, Australia has been slow to respond. State legislation only began to be passed in 1997 and some might posit that activism around films such as *Bad Boy Bubby* encouraged government action. While humane societies are extremely active in the US, the system is open to neglect or even abuse because the responsibility of ensuring the presence of an AHA representative on set lies with one individual, the producer.

Thus far, I have examined *Bad Boy Bubby*'s experimental production and its initial festival success and attendant controversy. I have outlined the liberal censorship rules around film festival screenings and examined the Acts, laws and regulation bodies affecting censorship and ratings, and how they influenced the film's festival, rating and distribution history. The next section will take a different tack. Through close analysis of *Bad Boy Bubby*, particularly its first act, I hope to shed further light on whether the film did actually involve animal cruelty and why it produced such conflicting responses in audiences and critics alike.

# ✖ PART 4

KEY SCENE ANALYSIS

## Huit Clos

*Bad Boy Bubby* opens on a widescreen close-up image of the face of a man in his mid-thirties. It's a strong face with intense eyes, shoulder-length hair cut blunt and thinning on top. We see two fleshy arms with plump hands smearing shaving cream across the man's cheeks and chin. The camera begins to pan out, revealing that the arms belong to a dour elderly woman, who starts to shave the man's cheeks with a metal razor. He flinches and she smartly slaps him on the side of the head demanding, 'Be still!' He sits still, staring off into the distance with slightly glazed eyes. In the background there is the constant buzz of an industrial, mechanical soundscape; the hiss of wires and the screech of metal on metal create the sense of an external world, separate to this room. As the opening titles continue, we cut to a medium shot, really an establishing shot of the place in which we will spend the first act (around thirty-five minutes) of this film – a grey, greasy, dingy two-room flat-come-cell, with dull filtered light and sweat-stained walls and floors. To the right of the room, the same man stands in a metal laundry tub, naked, while the elderly woman bends before him, giving him a sponge bath (see Figure 4). He stands as if dazed, arms stiffly raised. There is a makeshift alcove kitchen behind the two figures. A couple of shelves hold basic supplies, tins of tea and sugar, a bottle of cheap McWilliam's sherry. Set high on the back wall is a barred and grimy window. To the left side of the room is a small round table with two mismatched chairs. As the woman moves around to wash the man's back, the title *Bad Boy Bubby* appears in large white letters like a banner across the screen. We could be in a Depression-era war bunker or a 'mental' institution, for at this point in the film nothing is clear.

The sequence continues with a medium shot of the man, his hair freshly combed, sitting patiently at the small round table, the grime of the

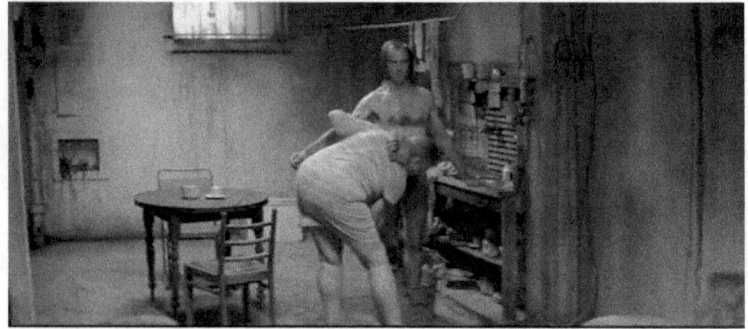

Figure 4: The woman (Mom), the man (Bubby) and the room.

room even more evident. On the stove a kettle boils, while the man, his face in shadows, steals furtive glances at the elderly woman, who stands with her back to him in the righthand foreground of the frame, her dress pulled down around her waist, washing her ample upper body. The kettle boils, he gets up, all the while watching the woman as he moves towards her, grabs a tin bowl from the shelf beside her and, never taking his eyes off her, returns to the table. She continues to wash as if oblivious to his movements. He sits back down at the table, waiting, obedient, like some kind of pet. Next we see an extreme close-up of the tin bowl. The man's hands rest either side of the bowl in a pose repeated many times throughout this opening sequence. Again in close-up, we see the woman's fingers ripping up pieces of white bread and dropping them into the bowl. We cut to a medium shot of the man as his lips curve with a slight smile when the woman begins to sprinkle some sugar on the bread. The camera pans up to her face as she steps away from the table to grab something from the stove. We see her in profile but we are yet to really see her, for at this point the framing has atomized all of her actions into a play of short ritualized gestures. Finally, we see her expressionless face looking down as she pours the milk and in a two-shot we see the man looking up at her with a timid smile, suggesting a level of affection.

The way in which the camera has captured these small gestures in close-up images is suggestive of the restrictions of this environment. As we begin to learn more about the man, we understand that these two rooms are his world and that the everyday rituals of washing and eating break the monotony, while also hinting at the stunted nature of his personal development. He is unsocialized. Yet that small smile he has for the elderly woman and the way in which his eyes follow her actions imply a deeper relationship than the sanitised gestures would suggest. While we might not want to call it love, we can see that this is a relationship of dependence and care. We don't know as yet what the relationship is between the man and woman, but she looks after all of his needs and is the centre of his world.

The woman then pours warm milk on the bread and sugar and the man eagerly begins to eat, with the enthusiasm of a child. The opening credit titles continue as we zoom slowly in on a shot of the two of them, facing each other. She sits still on the right of the frame, as he applies her mascara. He takes the cap off a lipstick and winds it up to reveal the colour, drops his gaze and looks at it as the camera slowly moves in and pans slightly left, revealing the concentration on his face as he repeats the words 'Princess Pink' in an automaton's voice. Finding the right lipstick, he begins to apply it. His voice suggests that he is perhaps autistic or that something very 'strange' is going on here and that he has been drugged or even lobotomized. He focuses as he applies the woman's lipstick. The two-shot with the slight camera move to reframe the focus of the action is characteristic of de Heer's style. In a Q & A session held after the Australian release of his feature film *The King Is Dead* on 12 July 2012 in Melbourne, he explained that for him the 'shoot is all about performance'. The signature slight movement and shift of the camera to refocus on an individual character's actions is the director's way of ensuring that performance is primary.

We next see a medium shot of the woman in profile sipping a cup of tea while on the soundtrack we hear what sounds like a cat purring. We cut to the man, perched on the edge of a wooden box with a wire lid. With his hands clasping his knees, he leans over and peers inside the box. A close-up overhead shot reveals a black-and-white cat hissing as he pokes a stick at it. It is the treatment of this cat that provoked most of the controversy surrounding *Bad Boy Bubby*. Over approximately the next ten minutes, we witness what appear to be numerous instances of the man tormenting the cat. Strangely enough, as the man's tendency towards repetition becomes more evident, we find him not only repeating the woman's speech but the sounds the cat makes and its actions. In his mimicry of the world, he does not discriminate between animal and human.

## Cockroaches

In the next scene we see the elderly woman placing paper cupcake cases on a tray; the key light illuminating her whitish-grey hair and the beige-and-off-white striped fabric of her dress. The lighting focuses attention on her methodical slow actions in this drab, bleak room. She is oblivious to the man who crawls past her on all fours as she pours toffee into the cupcake cases. He crawls, hops and scurries to the other side of the room, which contains a heavy, dark, patterned lounge suite from a bygone era. Crawling on the ground, he grabs at an old skirting board, pulling it from the wall. An extreme close-up reveals several cockroaches, one of which he tries to grab with his hand. A low-angle shot focuses on his face, a picture of concentration as he attempts to capture the pests. All the while in the foreground of the room, the elderly woman, engrossed in her actions, systematically continues to pour toffee into the cupcake cases, failing to respond to the man's bizarre actions as he prances and jumps around the room. We are then faced with a close-up image of a cockroach lying on its back. Panning right to left, the camera slowly reveals an extended trail of cockroach legs and then stops on a close-up of the man's eyes and part of his face (see Figure 5). With his fingers he pokes at a legless but still living cockroach as it wobbles from side to side. None of the reviews of *Bad Boy Bubby* mentions what happens to the cockroaches: all the attention

Figure 5: Bubby plays with the 'amputated' legs of a cockroach.

revolves around the treatment of the cat. Insect rather than animal, the cockroach is generally not considered worthy of our concern because we think of it as a germ-ridden scuttling pest; whereas the cat, even if feral, reminds us of our domestic pets. The scene is powerful in the way in which it suggests the character suffers some kind of pathology whereby the moronic but cruel dismembering of insects seems normal. In fact, the man plays with the cockroach in the same way that a well-fed cat will toy with its prey. In his autobiography, Nicholas Hope describes the scene with the cockroaches:

> Confessor Caresser Tim has been sitting all morning quietly cutting the insects' legs off with scissors, and I am disturbed at the sight and the actuality. It's something I don't really approve of. I hover around, trying to think of ways of avoiding the scene. 'Do you think they feel pain?' I ask primly. 'Nah,' says Tim, 'we put them in the freezer first.' This makes me feel better. When the time comes, I have no problem playing with the dismembered, slowly thawing insects until we get the shot. The cat is harder. (2004, p. 21)

Public outrage about the poor treatment of animals generally focuses on cruelty to mammals; however in scrolling through social-network communities advocating animal rights, this hierarchy appears to be less apparent. For example, in a debate on the Animal Rights Community website on 'Movies to Avoid' due to scenes of animal cruelty, there is a virtual sigh of relief from one contributor on discovering that a scene in *Starship Troopers* (1997) showing cockroaches being squashed actually used fakes. Yet, in relation to *Bad Boy Bubby*, the focus is always on the cat. Another posting about the film mentioned the number of entries on the news board of the IMDb (International Movie Database) link that seemed dismissive of the treatment of the cat:

> Having seen this film many years ago and never seen it since it really left its mark on me (http://www.imdb.com/title/tt0106341/board/nest/31492021) If you haven't clicked the link it is a film called 'bad boy bubby' the scene with a cat wrapped up in cling film i found completely distressing, some of the posts in the above thread seem quite dismissive of the animals anguish, having watched it there was no way in my eyes that this scene was simulated. (2006)

So even when such a forum considers the film, it is generally all about the cat.

## Incest and Fear

After the cockroach sequence, we then see the man again poking a stick into the wire-topped, wooden box containing the cat, while on the soundtrack we hear the sounds of purring. We cannot help but think at this point in the film that these are the shocking games of a demented child – in this case a man-child. Then it is night time and a single, stark electric bulb illuminates a room as we see the naked torso of the elderly woman, head thrown back, her back arched, whispering, 'Such a beautiful boy, such a beautiful boy', while she rocks backwards and forwards. 'That's right', she says as a smile animates her face for the first time. 'Good boy, Bubby', she coos as the camera pans down to reveal the much younger man's hands caressing her large pendulous breasts, as he lies still on the bed beneath her. It is a revealing moment, vividly illustrating how the older women has infantilized the man as a 'bubby' – and that the relationship of carer/receiver is also a sexual one. Our disorientation continues as the next swift edit returns us to the man sitting at the small round kitchen table. The woman is dressed in a different grey dress, her neatly combed hair pulled back in a ponytail, leather bag clasped in her hand. She places two toffees in between the palms of the man we now know as Bubby and demands in a stern voice, 'Toilet?' With a slight nod of his head he registers he is fine and in a threatening voice she demands, 'Don't move.' Pointing to the righthand wall while still looking at him, she hisses, 'Jesus can see everything. If he tells me you've moved, by Christ, I'll beat you brainless.' She then walks towards the heavy wooden door at the back of the room. In a medium close-up from the lefthand side of the frame, we see her use a large key to unlock the door. She reaches up to the wall beside the door and grabs a gas mask that looks like a relic from a past world war. Donning the mask, she unbolts the door and opens it, turning to yell once more, 'Be still!' before she closes it and we hear the sounds of the key turning, locking Bubby in, and then her footsteps slowly becoming fainter until they disappear. The camera cuts back to Bubby, isolated, a captive of his carer, of the fear of 'Jesus', of this miserable dank, dark cell. Initially, he sits as if paralysed, too scared to move. The length of time in which we linger on this shot compounds the sense of Bubby's fearfulness – of the fear that prevents him from moving. A slight reframing again shows Bubby sitting at the table, his back to the door.

Eventually, he picks up a toffee and, delicately peeling back the cupcake paper, slowly begins to eat it. The next image is of him still sitting motionless at the table with his hands placed flat on the tabletop, the shredded toffee wrappers between them. The camera cuts to a shot of a headless Christ on a crucifix hanging high on a grimy grey wall and then pans back down to Bubby sitting at the table looking up. He then stares straight ahead, his jaws clenched and a look of extreme concentration on his face. The camera focuses on his seated form and then slowly pans down to the legs of the chair as we see urine leaking onto the floor. We begin to understand something about his mindset. Bubby truly believes in an omniscient god, his fear of whom paralyses him to the point of soiling himself. In this scene we begin to understand that he is a victim of both sexual and psychological abuse. He continues to sit at the table, drenched in his own urine. Shadows flicker across the room as the day passes; night comes and he continues to sit still, now in darkness. Finally, we hear the sound of someone at the door and his mother returns. In the background of the frame, she switches on a light and takes off the gas mask, while in the foreground the single lightbulb now illuminates Bubby's face. He sits with his head slightly bowed, his clown-like hair giving him the appearance of a tragicomic figure. Under his dark brows, his eyes appear red-rimmed and watery. His strong, wide mouth is clenched tight and his body shakes slightly as he waits for her approach. Almost in tears, he whimpers in a child's voice, 'Bubby naughty'. Noticing he has soiled himself, she shoves him and swears. The camera ensures our focus is still on Bubby. In a medium close-up shot he is centre frame and we are aligned with his experience. The elderly woman hits him across the back and shoulders, cursing him as 'filthy' until he begins to cry. The next image is one of cruel humiliation. In a wide-angle, close-up shot, we see Bubby standing with his back to us. All we really see are the edge of his top, his naked bottom and the top of his thighs. In part shadow, the woman leans in front of him scrubbing him clean, wiping between his legs with a cloth. Then from a low angle, we look up to a head-and-shoulder shot of Bubby. There is a single lightbulb to the left of the frame and the barred window to the right. Bubby, his face tense, again stands still, yet his body sways with the vigorousness of the woman's washing. His eyes are raised and the direction of his gaze suggests that he is perhaps looking toward the headless Christ in anger, humiliation – shame. We then cut to another sex scene, the woman again astride him, as she rocks, she coos: 'You are such a good little boy …. Mummy does love little Bubby.' It is a shock when the nature of their relationship is finally confirmed: she is his captor, abuser, lover – and mother. However, while audiences and critics may have found the action in these scenes bizarre, offensive and bleak, most of the controversy focused on the next scene, in which Bubby, dressed as his mother, re-enacts the offences and indignities he regularly suffers on his imprisoned cat.

## It's All about the Cat

From a low angle we look at a scene that feels like a stage set. Framed by the greasy, stained walls of the cell, Bubby stands in the background, centre of frame. He is dressed in his mother's 'good' grey dress – the one she wears when she ventures out into the world. He has padded the dress, simulating her large, pendulous breasts. His lips are bright with her lipstick, and he holds a wooden spoon in his hand. Bubby stands with his arms by his sides, looking down at the cat, which appears to be tied by a cord around its neck to one of the chairs by the small table where he normally eats. In a frenzy, the black-and-white cat struggles to free itself, but its movement is restricted by the cord around its neck (see Figure 6). The hair on the cat's tail is puffed up; physical evidence that it feels threatened. Bubby stands at attention watching the cat's struggle. The cat's body contorts as it jumps up and down on the chair, causing it to rock precariously backwards and forwards. The next cut reveals Mom in the dark corner of the kitchen cooking something on the stove, while in voiceover

Figure 6: In role play as his mother, Bubby watches the cat's frenzied actions.

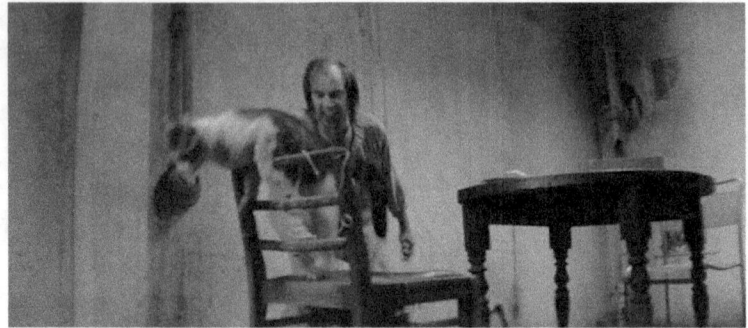

Figure 7: Bubby snarls while the cat struggles to escape.

we hear Bubby command the cat to 'Be still!' In perfect mimicry of his mother's intonation, he repeats the all-too-familiar phrase as we continue to hear the agitated sound of the chair rocking. We cut back to the chair where we see the cat with its head and forepaws over the top of the chair (see Figure 7), desperately trying to pull itself free. A now animated Bubby bends forward and snarls, 'Be still, be still, be still you little cunt.' By now the chair is on a tilt and the cat, with flattened ears, has returned to its seat, and appears somewhat calmed as Bubby again leans towards it and quietly states, 'By Christ I'll beat you brainless.' Leaning in even closer towards the cat, which continues to attempt to pull away from the cord that binds it, he whispers, 'Can't go outside because no gas mask.' In a theatrical flourish, he then yells, 'And Bubby die!', coughing and spluttering as if he can't breathe. The cat continues to sit still on the chair, crouched, its hair raised. Again Bubby tells the cat to be still, then turns and in a determined manner walks towards the door. Acting as if to leave, he grabs the gas mask and places it on his head. Then taking the mask off, he gasps, 'Poison' as he begins to collapse, as if suffering the deadly effects of a toxic atmosphere. The camera cuts back to his mother, who is still cooking; she chimes in with her words of wisdom opining, 'If the poison don't get you' and, like an obedient schoolboy who has done his homework, Bubby responds, 'Then God will!'

In Bubby's role play, he places the cat in his position of entrapment and submission. In his limited world, mimicry is his only means of exchange, engagement and learning. His mother's behaviour is entirely perfunctory except at night when her sexual requirements generate some warmth towards him. Otherwise, Bubby is trapped in this cell, fearful of the outside world and desperate for affection and love. Generally, what happens on set is not the same as what we see on screen; rather the film is completed through the technology of editing and special effects. However, in this case, what we see is what happened on set. This part of the scene was not censored and it is still extremely uncomfortable for an audience to watch the cat's obvious distress. However, it is the next part in which 'Bubby maltreats the cat ... where he sits by [the] kitchen table pulling the cat to him hard round its neck' (see Figure 8) that the BBFC removed before first releasing the film (Green, 2011).

The torment resumes, with Bubby now sitting in one of the lounge chairs in his pyjamas pulling the cat towards him by the cord around its neck. The cat attempts to pull away from its tormentor but Bubby keeps dragging it closer (see Figure 8), hissing at it. The action continues, with Bubby letting the cat run to the full length of the cord before he reels it back in as it resists by extracting its claws and grasping the carpet beneath it (see Figure 9). All the while in the background his mother continues to prepare some meagre meal.

Figure 8: Bubby pulls the cat towards him by a cord as it attempts to resist.

Figure 9: As Bubby pulls the cord, the cat claws at the carpet.

The scene continues with Bubby asking in a mechanical voice, 'Where cat from?' Mom responds in a dull tone, 'Outside.' We cut to a close-up, wide-angle shot of Bubby's face, captured mid-concentration, with a slightly devilish look in his eyes. Sounding puzzled, he asks his mother, 'How come he no gas mask?' From behind him, continuing to stir something on the stove, she replies in a monosyllabic way, 'Don't need it, don't breathe.' Bubby seems to ponder this new fact and, with the curiosity of a child, asks, 'How then breathe?' In response, she leaves her cooking, walks up behind him, grasps him around the head and places her hand firmly over his mouth, clenches his nostril passages shut with her other hand and begins to suffocate him. In a medium close-up shot, we see him submit to her actions, initially just blinking, not really moving. She rests her chin against his head as she firmly holds him until the lack of air finally sends him into a panic and he begins to struggle. But Mom just grimaces and holds him tighter as the camera pulls back to reveal the two of them in the middle of the room, his legs splayed and struggling, as he tries to rip her hands from his mouth. All the while he holds the cord at the end of which is the cat trying to pull away from the struggling figures (see Figure 10). Finally, she lets him go and returns to her cooking, explaining in a perfunctory way, 'That's not breathing', as if she has just given her child a mundane lesson. She then turns and dumps some food on the table saying, 'Eat.' In the foreground of the frame, Bubby sits looking slightly

Figure 10: Mom demonstrates to Bubby how it feels not to breathe, while he still holds the cord tied around the cat's neck.

stunned, his longish hair dishevelled, trying to assess the lesson he has learned, as he gulps in large mouthfuls of air.

When we look at these representations out of context, as singular images rather than frames within a scene within a film, it is difficult to remain unemotional about the distress caused to the cat. But this is what the classification board must do to make an objective assessment. As previously noted, with regard to the Animal Act, rating and censorship boards need to decide whether the scenes 'involved the cruel infliction of pain and terror on an animal or the cruel goading of an animal to fury'. The BBFC's election to reconsider the scene, however, was partly informed by further supporting documentation from the distributor and the director de Heer, reassuring the board of the well-being of the cats on set. As previously noted, de Heer confirmed that the film fully conformed to the legislation for the handling of animals in film (Green, 2011). Yet the treatment of the cat has haunted the production, with both the main character and the director continually being asked to justify these scenes. Discussing what happened on set, Hope says:

> Bubby has a cat, which he unknowingly traumatises and then kills by accident. Our studio cat has been taken from an animal shelter's death row for feral cats. It has to be killed unless it finds a home. Our cat will be

> looked after for the few days it is on set, then returned to the vet and killed. We will then use the dead body.
> 
> In between times, I'm meant to make the cat hiss and spit. This isn't so hard: it spits and hisses most of the time. It's scared. It's probably spent all its life spitting and hissing. We get to a scene where the cat is tied to a chair for Bubby to shout at it. It's pretty calm about being tied up. It sits quietly through the rehearsal. But once the camera starts, the cat goes crazy. It tries to get off the chair but can't because of the ropes. It panics. The cat is so frantic the chair nearly falls over. I wonder if I should stop the scene, try to calm the cat down. But I also know how good this looks on camera, and I know no one can get near the animal anyway. It's too wild. So I carry on … .
> 
> We have more scenes to do with the cat, but Rolf is traumatised. 'I feel like an SS man,' he says. 'We have to stop.' We all agree. We feel terrible. We can't go the extra step of putting the cat through more scenes. So we send it to the vet. (2004, pp. 21–2)

In Australia, urban stray and feral cats are trapped and captured by council pounds and animal leagues. If a cat is feral, it is generally destroyed in a humane way. Attempts are made to find homes for stray cats that are comfortable with human contact, but many of these are also destroyed. The hissing and spitting of the black-and-white cat and its reluctance to be handled by humans would suggest it was feral and therefore going to be killed. Yet I would argue that, even though the cat was feral, due to new regulations passed in the last decade by most states in Australia outlining the appropriate treatment of animals in media, it would be very difficult to get similar scenes past the censors now. Clearly, the treatment of the cat has had an effect on Hope who, during publicity tours for the DVD release of the film in 2005, stated that these days he never works with animals (Hope, 2010).

It is the next scene, however, that precipitated the Italian controversy, occasioning appeals to the President of Italy, Oscar Luigi Scalfaro, to suspend screenings. These came from the regional councillor of the Italian Green

Figure 11: Bubby with the cling-wrapped cat.

Party, Michele Boato, who believed that a cat had been tortured to death during the making of the film. *Bad Boy Bubby* is a confrontational film but this scene is particularly shocking, for we see Bubby, again in a medium close-up shot, with the same black-and-white cat completely encased in cling wrap, except for its head. He sits at the kitchen table holding the cat like a swaddled baby (see Figure 11), and begins to experiment with its breathing. He appears to place his hand across the cat's nose; its ears are laid back, again, generally a physical sign that it feels threatened. All the while the industrial soundtrack pumps out a beat, like a clock counting down, as the camera remains motionless on Bubby and the cat – as we, in anticipation, anxiously hold our breath. We later see the cat back in its box, surprisingly unharmed. The long drawn-out focus on images or repetitive activities further conveys the boredom and constraints of Bubby's imprisonment. The next shot shows him sitting at the table playing with some cling wrap and his own breathing. Placing the wrap across his face, the camera captures his blurred features and we sense the restriction of his breathing. He seems repeatedly surprised as he rips the plastic from his mouth when his body starts to fight for air. At one point we see his mother sitting opposite him, drinking sherry and visibly drunk. She gets up and decides to go out but forgets to play the usual charade and leaves her gas mask behind. Bubby continues to amuse himself with the cling wrap. Then we are confronted with a truly macabre image of the same

Figure 12: The entombed dead cat.

cat completely mummified in cling wrap (see Figure 12). It appears as though Bubby's experiments with breathing have finally resulted in the animal's death. But death is also something that Bubby doesn't really understand, as will become more clearly evident later in this first act, after he has suffocated his drunken parents with cling wrap. He sits patiently with his tin plate waiting for his mother to make him something to eat, seemingly oblivious to the actuality of death. In this absurdist, black moment, he hisses at the dead cat, shakes it, slaps it and seems completely bewildered by its failure to respond. Eventually, he unwraps the cling wrap from the cat's head, and we can see that it is the same cat and that it is truly dead. In the midst of his inspection of the dead cat, someone knocks on the door. Bubby is so shocked that he drops the corpse and sits rigid in his seat. From now on Bubby's world will radically change and enlarge, first with the introduction of his father and then his eventual escape to the 'outside' world and a kaleidoscope of new experiences.

It is almost impossible to imagine how anyone could manage to encase any cat in cling wrap, let alone a stray or feral one. While specific details are not forthcoming here, one assumes that the cat was tranquillized. It is easy to understand how back in 1994 the Italian Green Party councillor could believe that a cat had actually been suffocated to death on screen and feel moved to demand further screenings of the film be halted. But even without the supporting documentation supplied by the distributor and de Heer, an examination of the film is enough to reveal that the actual suffocation of the cat is never shown, with Hope only ever appearing to put his hands on the cat's nose and mouth. But we do know from information supplied by the producer, de Heer and actors and crew on the production, that the Animal Welfare League of South Australia supplied the two cats featured in the film and was responsible for euthanizing the feral cat.

On the DVD Audio Commentary to the Umbrella release of the film, both de Heer and Hope claim the cat purred continuously while it was bound in cling wrap. However, they also noted that some of the crew were deeply disturbed when the Animal Welfare League supplied the carcass of the same cat for use in this scene. The league had first euthanized it and then removed its organs (2010a). As a feral cat it would, most likely, have been destroyed anyway but whether this justifies the distress that it probably experienced during the shoot is another matter entirely.

Furthermore, this was not the only cat used in the film – there were in fact two live ones and the body of a third. Once Bubby kills his parents and escapes his cell, he takes up residency in a junk pile on the wharves and adopts a grey tabby kitten. The kitten is obviously domesticated and allows Bubby to hold and pet it. Unaware of any other form of interaction than the master/captive dynamic established with his mother, Bubby resorts to the only form of expression he knows by yelling at the kitten, 'Be still, you little bastard!' Whether due to the kitten's plaintive mews or because it is sweet and small – a baby – he begins to temper the aggression of his address. He leaves the kitten to search for food only to return and find that a group of thugs have beaten it to death. The sequence is shot in such a way that we never see the impact of the blows on the kitten. What we do see is what appears to be its dead body as Bubby picks up its slack form, holds it to his cheek and mournfully strokes it. The next day he sits in a park with the carcass of a cat lying across his lap, while he eats pizza and again comes across Angel and Rachael. On both the Audio Commentary and in the interview 'Christ Kid: You're a Weirdo' included on the DVD and Blu-ray release of the film, de

Heer and Hope confirm that a veterinarian, who was present on set, put the kitten to sleep for a very short period of time. They also confirm it lived a long and happy life after being adopted by Claire Benito. (This outcome also enables de Heer to claim that a cat was actually saved through the making of the film.) We are only ever given a very brief glimpse of the carcass of the cat on Bubby's lap while he sits in the park. While it is supposed to be the body of his kitten, it is obviously not as it has ginger patches and is possibly a tortoiseshell. The director claims that the crew found the dead and beheaded body of a kitten in a park near where they were working, so they used it in the shoot. This explains why the carcass we see is barely shown in the frame. De Heer has said that the 'stuff with the cats was all worked out very carefully. We had a vet and animal welfare people on set .... There is a feral cat eradication program going in Australia and we borrowed a feral cat.' As I have previously noted, although the director has apologized for the degree of suffering the black-and-white cat might have endured, he also believes it to have been 'infinitesimal compared to real issues that beset the world'. Yet, when I think of that beheaded kitten in the park, I cannot help but be reminded of Animal Liberation Victoria representative Rheya Linden's words when she states, 'There is a lot of prejudice towards cats in the community and I think filmmakers need to be careful depicting cruelty to cats' (Zwar, 1998, p. 19).

During the film, we instinctively know that what is happening to the cat is real, while what is happening to Bubby is dramatic action. Yet in this film, breathing becomes a symbol not just of living – being able to breathe – but life itself, of what makes a good life. As previously discussed, cruelty towards animals is often considered the precursor to further aberrant behaviour. In *Bad Boy Bubby*, de Heer presents this cruelty as an example of the way in which he believes human beings, specifically children, are capable of change. A badly treated child will not always become an abusive adult; love, care and friendship can turn the world around and transform us.

# Part 5

## KEY THEMES

Having murdered his parents, Bubby then escapes the cell-like hovel he has called home for the thirty-five years of his life. From the *huit clos* of the first act of the film we move into a world of kaleidoscopic exchanges that take us on a journey, one in which everything Bubby sees, feels and breathes is new. It is a surprisingly beautiful but also cruel transition, which begins with pizza, beer and sex with a nubile member of the Salvation Army, but also results in him being beaten by a cop, kicked by feminists and sodomized by a prison inmate. In the final act of the film, Bubby finds some kind of cure in a psycho-dramatic performance of his traumatic life, fronting an alternative punk band (see Figure 13). On stage dressed as the adult Pop, rapping in a crazed mimicry-style monologue to an enraptured crowd, his moves animate the erotic actions of his sexual encounters, and the erratic movements of the occupants of the group house for the severely impaired who have allowed him to share their home. He ultimately finds love through a saviour – Angel – a carer rather than a

Figure 13: Fronting the alternative punk band, Bubby dressed as Pop, performs a psycho-dramatic rap of his traumatic life.

messenger of god, who acts as a kind of intermediary between his asocial and the social world.

De Heer is frequently called on in interviews and panels to discuss how and why *Bad Boy Bubby* became such a phenomenon. Interestingly, however, while there has been sustained research around the film's experimental nature, particularly its use of sound, less attention has been paid to its themes of disability, familial relations and innocence. This is surprising as, in the case of disability, the film was extremely progressive for the period in which it was made. Before addressing the key themes, I will first return to a discussion of the way in which the film was labelled as controversial in the media.

## Media Outrage and Criminal Associations

I have already acknowledged the accolades that the film, a natural focal point for the media, received at festivals and during its initial release but generally, responses to the work were diverse. Writing for the *Vancouver Sun*, Peter Birnie states: 'You want weird? ... Australia's *Bad Boy Bubby* is sure to be a festival hit with its blend of surreal sickness and belly laughs' (1994). Similarly, in the *Independent*, Sheila Johnston claims the film 'contains much wild, bad-taste and highly original comedy' (1994). Nigel Andrews bemoaned the circumstances that resulted in *Bad Boy Bubby* being released in London at the same time as a film by Ken Loach:

> What fine kismet decided that *Bad Boy Bubby* should open in the same week as *Ladybird, Ladybird*? Rolf de Heer's black Australian comedy ... is about an emotionally arrested young man (Nicholas Hope) escaping from decades of house arrest under a mercilessly 'loving' Mum. This fat old crone – the sort of mother Loach's Maggie might turn into given a minor increase in her possessive hysteria – has kept Junior at home as her pet, her baby, her lover. And home is a surreal, Beckettian hell of grey walls, mouldering food and free-range cockroaches. Watch Bubby

eat one; watch actor Hope do it for real. … But De Heer has a catchy Candide humour. He is soon staging witty confrontations between his all-innocent wild child and the special-interest groups that run planet earth. Bubby brings his perceptual innocence and untutored morals to the Salvation Army, a grunge rock group, a cerebral palsy ward. The film turns from horror comedy to satire, and the change is so deft that we hardly notice when it happens. (1994)

In the *Sun Herald*, Rob Lowing suggests: 'IF YOU want to see the most damning indictment of Australia yet – and most people may prefer something a little lighter – then *Bad Boy Bubby* is your film'; he goes on to observe: 'this is a brilliant and savage satire on the "ugly Australian": foul-mouthed drunken men and women who abuse their children and each other' (1994).

Many of the negative reviews have little substance, but what they have in common is a level of outrage at the film's subject matter. Writing for the *Independent* John Lyttle suggests that, '*Bad Boy Bubby* makes *Henry: Portrait of a Serial Killer* look like the Teddy Bears' Picnic' (1993), while Iain Johnstone claims:

The Australasians know that sensation is a passport to the international circuit. … *Bad Boy Bubby*, recently opened in London, is certainly shocking enough, with the eponymous Bubby having intercourse with his mother, being buggered by a prison inmate and finding fame as a rap star. It is also shockingly bad. (1994)

Lim Li Min's comments are, however, more extensive – and more damning. Having interviewed de Heer at the 1997 Singapore Film Festival, he suggests that what comes to mind while watching the film is:

*A Clockwork Orange*'s Alex, whose eyes, pried open by pincers, is [sic] forced to goggle a screen for hours on end. Although *Bad Boy Bubby* doesn't induce the same level of projectile vomiting, its subject matter;

> a dysfunctional mother-and-son pair whose relationship is in equal parts abusive and incestuous isn't exactly *Five Go on an Adventure* material. And the fact that its first half is claustrophobically played out in this tiny shoebox of a room which is bedroom/lounge/kitchen to both mother and son is enough to make you want to run, screaming, from the cinema hall.

In fact, the film did induce reviewer Mark Kermode, writing for the *Sunday Mail* (Glasgow), to exit the cinema, 'I walked out of a film festival when they screened the 1993 Australian film *Bad Boy Bubby* in which they mistreated a cat' (2012). It is the only film he mentions having walked out of in his entire career. The intensity of the film's impact generates curiosity which has kept it in the public eye and helped bring it to the attention of new audiences. In response to a discussion on banned films in the *Belfast Telegraph* in 2010, a reader felt compelled to write into the 'Comment' section stating: 'If you really want to see a non-banned film that is frightening and offensive check out *Bad Boy Bubby*. … Please be aware that this film is seriously twisted.' In searching through reviews that mention the film, we find it consistently labelled as 'offensive', 'violent' and 'shocking', but most authors spend barely more than a sentence on explaining the reasons for their outrage. Perhaps the lack of detailed analysis reflects on the state of press film criticism or, as I have previously noted, the level of neglect may be due to an inability to crystallize the complex and boundary-breaking subject matter of the film. Reviewers and audiences alike felt troubled by their responses to the film.

The film also attracted attention when on occasion the media drew parallels between aspects of its plot and contemporary criminal cases. In 1997, in what was referred to as a 'copy-cat crime', *Bad Boy Bubby* was mentioned in a broad range of Australian newspapers in the context of a murder involving cling wrap. Nineteen-year-old Troy David Keyte was sentenced to life imprisonment for murdering his girlfriend, seventeen-year-old Natasha Mahon, in their home in Rockingham, Western Australia on 20 September 1995. At the time of the murder, Keyte was only seventeen. Major and local newspapers across the country reported on the crime and Keyte's sentencing.

Keyte, who had experienced a very disturbing family life, acknowledged having seen *Bad Boy Bubby* and considered it a 'good' film. Fuelled by an obsessive jealousy and fearing that his girlfriend was about to leave him, Keyte decided to kill her by wrapping her head in cling wrap while she slept. The *Herald Sun* reported the Crown prosecutor Bruno Flannaca's statement that Keyte 'was inspired to murder Ms Mahon "in such a bizarre manner" by the Australian film *Bad Boy Bubby*, in which a character kills two others by wrapping their heads in plastic wrap' (Anonymous, 1997, p. 13). It seems terribly unfortunate that a film with such a humanist heart should be referenced in a murder trial and it is important to remember that, while Keyte mimicked Bubby's technique, his murderous intentions were born of mental illness.

An entirely different perspective on this film's relation to a crime can be found in Nicholas Hope's recollection of a particular meeting with some fans, recounted in his autobiography and numerous interviews. While in the tough mining town of Lightning Ridge, northern New South Wales, working on another film project, he was recognized by a couple of men in the bar of the hotel where he was staying. They told him that *Bad Boy Bubby* 'was the town's favourite film' and invited him to share a drink with them. Although feeling a little vulnerable in this macho environment, Hope agreed. He did, however, think it was strange that several of the men kept describing the film as 'a real Australian film about a real Australian family'. Eventually one of the men revealed that he and his brother had suffered extreme abuse as children, having been imprisoned by their father in a cage kept in the loft. The father would often only lower the cage from the loft for the brothers to see him abuse and torture their mother. Hope recalled that the brothers commented that, when their father died, the town threw the biggest party ever (2010). There is no official or media evidence of this crime, so we can only take the brothers' story at face value. But assuming it is the truth, one cannot help but wonder how many of the townspeople knew of the abuse and failed to stop it. We can only guess that for these brothers *Bad Boy Bubby* became like a beacon of shared experience and hope – that they, like Bubby had managed to survive the horror of their imprisonment by a parent in the 'family home'.

We can, however, confirm the facts of the appalling case of entrapment and sexual abuse inflicted by Austrian father, Josef Fritzl, on his daughter. My own response to this case was that it bore an uncanny resemblance to Bubby's entrapment and sexual and emotional abuse, a fact recognized by others:

> The horrific news story from Austria involving Josef Fritzl and the children he fathered by raping his daughter who he kept imprisoned in the basement of his house, sounds like the premise of some deranged movie. And it is … *Bad Boy Bubby*. (Schembri, 2008)

Bubby's circumstances had always seemed so unbelievable, but here we have a case of abuse and entrapment with eerie similarities. The notion of a 'room of one's own' takes on horrific connotations when we think about the *huit clos* of the film's first act and its marked similarity to the Fritzl criminal case. Media attention to this and other cases has shone new light on the film, bringing it to the notice of contemporary audiences, its surreal premise now having a touchstone in reality.

## Sons and Mothers

In the first act of *Bad Boy Bubby* our interest is entirely focused on Bubby and the woman who, it is slowly revealed, is his carer, captor, abuser, mother – and lover. Several authors have discussed the Oedipal nature of this relationship. He kills both his 'Pop' and 'Mom', and he replaces his mother with Angel, superficially a younger version of her with similarly large breasts and plump body. Commenting on the formation of Australian masculinity in the cinema of the 1990s, Rose Lucas discusses the parodic fashion in which the masculine as an Oedipal subject is played out in the film. Bubby is infantilised by his mother with whom 'he both enjoys and suffers an incestuous relationship' until their symbiotic relationship is disturbed by the return of Pop (1998, p. 144). Yet Lucas argues:

> Bubby may have broken the suffocating control of Mom; he may have taken on the power of Pop and have beaten him, enabling him to move on to relationships of caring and reciprocity – but he has had to murder to achieve this release, doing away with Angel's parents as well as his own. The scripts of the past constitute a heavy weight around the shoulders of this child-man, as he attempts to forge an image of self and of masculinity that is somehow unshackled, written from scratch. *Bad Boy Bubby* poses but cannot resolve the question of whether the Australian male can ever escape this dichotomy of only ever being Bubby or Pop, of only ever desiring Mom or Angel. (1998, p. 145)

Exploring mother-and-son relationships, where the maternal figure is dominant, in popular and cult cinema, Charles Jason Lee has also adopted a Freudian approach in studying the primary relationship in *Bad Boy Bubby*. Lee's reading of Bubby's character is one that suggests that he is unconstrained by 'societal boundaries after being enclosed all his life' (2005, p. 25). Lee claims that the film explores the way in which dehumanizing behaviour results from an 'inhuman wasteland', where Bubby is abused in several different situations. While Bubby's desire to see his parents making love is deemed as perverse by his father, in Freudian terms it is a normal part of development and individuation. Lee suggests that 'Bubby is Rousseau's noble savage crossed with the divine saviour figure' (2005, p. 26). Depicting an adult-child such as Bubby being 'abused' by his mother and desired by many, radically subverts notions of normality and confronts the conservative nature of Australian society (Lee, 2005, p. 25).

While the film does have a narrative synergy with the classic Oedipal story and Freudian interpretations (Bubby's desire for his mother, his killing of his father and his need to 'look' at his parents having sex), after the first act, it moves on to a different tack involving Bubby's developing social existence and his democratic acceptance of everyone he meets. Interestingly, one would expect the portrayal of such a mother to be damning, but de Heer refuses to simplify this relationship through easy stereotyping. It might make an audience feel uncomfortable, but there is sympathy here for Mom as well as a choice to demonstrate a shared affection between her and Bubby.

Throughout the opening act of the film, the images move in a disjointed way, capturing the monotony and bleakness of Bubby's life. The relationship that has now been established as mother and son – Bubby and Mom – is an abusive one. She beats him when he soils himself; she has convinced him that the outside world is toxic; and she uses him for sex. However, while she is both captor and abuser, she also appears to care for him. A single woman of no apparent means, she feeds and cleans her 'Bubby'. When his sleazy, drunken father arrives on the scene, disturbing Bubby's habitual, ritualized world and labelling him 'a weird one', she tries to explain away his idiosyncrasies and protect him. Although the sex scenes are disturbing, and we can never trivialize incest, because an adult male actor plays Bubby and because the sex appears to give him real pleasure, incest becomes normalized. We can then begin to understand Bubby's rage when his father usurps him in his mother's bed. For Bubby, the sex offers a release from the mind-numbing monotony of his captivity. It is only ever during sex that we hear his mother praise him in a soothing voice; otherwise she ignores him or fills him with fear about the outside world in order to ensure his continued entrapment. What we must consider, however, is that this bleak and miserable environment is primarily their shared world.

## Disability

While *Bad Boy Bubby* is a surreal gothic tale in the vein of some Eastern European cinema, when it comes to representing disability the film takes a social-realist turn. In an earlier section I discussed Heather Rose's work with Fred Stahl for the film she starred in and wrote with de Heer, *Dance Me to My*

*Song*. In the film, Rose, whose real name is Heather Slattery, plays Julia, a character who like herself suffers from cerebral palsy, a physical disability caused by an injury to the brain generally occurring *in utero*. While there can be mental retardation, the most common medical characteristics are involuntary movements, and disorders of posture and equilibrium (Cerebral Palsy Alliance website). Rose, who died in 2002, explained the focus of her film and how she ended up working with de Heer:

> One night I had a birthday party to which I invited Rolf. Fred and I talked about the script to Rolf, but Rolf didn't even want to read what we'd done so far, saying he didn't want to interfere with our process. A while later, Rolf called Fred at my place and asked him to come into the office. I had no idea what this could have been about. When Fred got back he told me Rolf wanted to help us develop the script further. This gave me a big boost in confidence, because it meant that someone really believed in me, in my ability to do something worthwhile, something that would benefit other people. (Vertigo Productions website)

On the Audio Commentary to the DVD release of *Bad Boy Bubby* de Heer describes the harsh circumstances of Rose's earlier years: consigned to a home by parents who considered her a 'vegetable', she spent the first eighteen years of her life in a crib with no view. The only people who ever bothered to speak to her directly were foreign cleaners working in the institution. In later life she fell in love with one of her carers, who was then swiftly transferred to a different area of the facility (2010a). Rose only makes a brief appearance in *Bad Boy Bubby*, but her personal story seems to inform the scenes that play out in the group house whose occupants open their door and their hearts to Bubby.

The first group-house scene involves Bubby participating in physical therapy, as the disabled inmates are gently touched and massaged, many of them cooing and sighing with pleasure. Bubby is now dressed as the authoritative Pop. After enduring numerous assaults, Bubby returns to the 'home' where he spent the first thirty-five years of his life. The police's white chalk outlines of his parents' bodies are still visible on the floor. Eventually, driven by hunger, he decides to confront the world again, but this time he presents himself with his father's clothes, priest collar and suitcase. It is as if Bubby thinks that, as his father came from the outside world, he might have a better chance of surviving in that world dressed as 'Pop'. Bubby has now found a life that alternates between his home with Angel at the group house and his nightly cathartic rants fronting the band.

The first group scene is shot in such a way as to take us into the social world of these people – as if we are participants in an actual therapy session. The carer's voice calmly intones a visual relaxation exercise while contorted bodies are gently manipulated, massaged and stroked. The scene appears as an antidote to Rose's own story of abandonment and isolation – of the complete lack of human contact. Within the context of *Bad Boy Bubby* this is also the place in which Bubby begins to develop the capacity for insight and empathy. Bubby has grown up in a situation where touch has been distorted into extremes of physical contact: being slapped, pushed and thumped by Mom and Pop, kicked by the feminists and beaten by a cop; being sexualized through his mother's incestuous actions or the violently abusive rape in the prison. Even the young Salvation Army woman promptly takes him to her bed, enchanting him with her singing. The scenes in the group home symbolize a powerful moment of healing, with Bubby's own awkward bodily movements soothed by the caring and sensual touch of others.

There is an extremely poignant scene at the home in which Bubby holds Rachael in his arms as they both weep copious tears. Earlier in the film when Bubby first arrives at the home, Rachael, in a bold move acknowledging her sexuality, something so often denied to a person with disabilities, suggests that he should stay in her room. Angel, their carer, agrees that Bubby should stay, but suggests that he stay with the men in their room. Cradling Rachael in his arms and gently rocking her, Bubby, in a tearful voice, explains that she has fallen in love with him. The problem is that, while Bubby cares for Rachael, he does not love her in a romantic way but has fallen in love with Angel. It is an intensely potent and anguished moment that speaks of a world of loss, suffering and pain. Possibly it intimates the terrible sadness Heather Rose must have felt when the man she loved was moved on to another ward to prevent her ever seeing him again.

Bubby himself is often perceived as a character in the grip of a kind of mental illness but in fact his idiosyncrasies result from abuse and, most significantly, from the fact that he has never been socialized. At the time of the film's release, mental illness and disability were gaining greater visibility on Australian and international screens, with films such as Polish-born Australian resident, Jerzy Domarodzki's *Struck by Lightning* (1990), which focuses on the introduction of experimental physical therapy for disabled young adults living in a shelter. His 1996 film *Lilian's Story*, based on Kate Grenville's 1985 novel, starred Toni Collette in the titular role as a woman who has been institutionalized by her father for forty years. Earlier examples include Jane Campion's *Sweetie*, whose main character's transgressive behaviour upset critics around the world and her 1990 film *An Angel at My Table*, which dealt with the life of the New Zealand writer, Janet Frame, who spent years in psychiatric hospitals. It is also during this period that Scott Hicks found international fame with *Shine* (1996), a biographical film about the pianist David Helfgott, who never fully recovered from a severe breakdown he suffered as a young man. In previous eras, mental illness and disability have been portrayed as afflictions that led individuals to be isolated, stigmatized or feared. The increasing visibility of disability in the 1990s reflected not only a growing awareness of mental illness and, to a lesser degree, disability on the part of society, but helped to shift attitudes from fear and ignorance towards greater understanding and even empathy. Katie Ellis has written extensively on the construction of disability in Australian national cinema, specifically during the 1990s, when this cinema was 'committed to serving underrepresented populations' (2008, p. 1). While a political and cultural push for diversity ensued, with a growing focus on minority ethnic, religious, sexual and gendered groups, disabled characters often functioned purely as representations of medical pathology, the disability becoming the focus of the film. Ellis writes:

> During the 1990s, the Disability Rights movement in Australia attempted to take the focus away from the traditional medical aspects of disability and concentrate instead on the contribution people could make to society. As a result, an environment emerged where we were encouraged to 'see the ability, not the disability'. While this framework removed the focus from medicine, it remained under the same ideological umbrella, since disability remained an individual's problem and disabled people were encouraged to deny their impairments in order to fit into an ableist society. Disability is a social construction. As a result, despite the focus on cultural diversity in Australian National Cinema during the 1990s, disability continued to be largely unproblematised. (2008, p. 2)

According to Ellis, until the 1990s the cinema had generally been an 'influential social barrier' for people with impairments (2008, p. 2). The way in which disability is represented in film functions as a cultural tool, which shapes perceptions. Social responsibility is a frequent narrative trope in many of de Heer's films, including *Dingo*, *Epsilon* (1997) and *The Tracker*. The social mode of disability 'reveals that power relations that surround the representation of disability in the cinema also shape disability'. Ellis further argues that *Bad Boy Bubby* is one of the few films of the period to reflect on the 'social constructions of disability' by introducing the topic to the storyline without aestheticizing the representation to make the film 'easier to watch' (2008, p. 95). While *Bad Boy Bubby* is not a film specifically about a character with disabilities, it explores how audiences and society alike perceive superficial appearances and pass judgement in an arbitrary way. As Ellis notes, because Bubby is unsocialized, he treats everyone as an equal; the film 'highlights identity as socially constructed and subverts many of the ableist myths' usually perpetuated by the cinema (2008, p. 99). Bubby's developing relationship with Rachael and his unquestioning acceptance highlights, according to Ellis, the way in which the film offers a 'critical understanding of disability as a construction through social norms and power dynamics' (2011, p. 107). Bubby is the only person who attempts to communicate directly with the people in the home. Even Angel, their carer, who is held up as a sympathetic figure with whom Bubby eventually falls in love and has a family, turns to him to translate their speech. Instead of allowing Bubby to choose whether to sleep in Rachael's room, Angel makes the decision for him. The film therefore works to create a disability identity that does not shy away from an impairment's actuality as seen in the therapy sessions, but nor does it isolate and fetishize the character. The severely impaired social characters are a part of the film's everyday world along with the alternative band, the Salvation Army and the patrons who frequent the pizza joint.

## Innocence

Audiences and critics alike have sought to find explanations in de Heer's life for the rawness and brutality of Bubby's story. The writer-director's bemused response to these frequent queries is to attest that he had a very happy childhood and comes from a loving and supportive family (Susskind, 1994, p. 82; de Heer, 1996, p. 7). Local Australian publisher, Currency Press, a company that operates out of Sydney, New South Wales, published the screenplay of the film several years after its release in 1996. The screenplay serves as a reference tool for screenwriters and as a teaching tool for scriptwriting and editing courses. In the published screenplay, de Heer ponders the provenance of the idea for *Bad Boy Bubby*'s man-child:

> 'Where did *that* come from?' This is a question I am often asked, either about parts of *Bad Boy Bubby* or about the whole of it – I usually answer with an 'I don't know'. The answer for the whole film is too long and complicated, and as for the individual parts, I often genuinely don't know. (1996, p. 7)

Yet he also acknowledges that his interest in childhood began much earlier in his life:

> I have travelled in the world of childhood since I was young. Children are a source of endless fascination, insight and inspiration, and, to me, childhood is the most precious of all things. In one form or another then, much of what I write and think about concerns childhood. ('Production Notes', Vertigo Productions website)

Looking back over the director's working history, it becomes apparent that themes like childhood, innocence and familial relations are central to many of his films. His first film, the children's feature *Tail of a Tiger*, revealed an early fascination with the wonder of childhood. In 1996, several years after *Bad Boy Bubby* was made, *The Quiet Room* (1996) premiered in competition at the Cannes Film Festival and went on to become one of de Heer's most financially successful films. The director had had children in the ten years or so that it took for *Bad Boy Bubby* to evolve, and he claims the experience affected him deeply, changing him 'very much as a human being' (quoted in Malone, 2001b, p. 59). For the main role of the 'girl' in *The Quiet Room*, he cast his own daughters at different ages – Chloe as the girl at age seven and Phoebe as the girl at age three – a decision made partly to ensure he could spend more time with his family while working ('Production Notes', Vertigo Productions website). The film focuses on the girl's perceptions of the breakdown of her parents' relationship. Routine daily life continues as usual but she knows something is not quite right. Things have changed and the happiness, joy and love that imbued her family life when she was a three-year-old seem to have disappeared. The parents say nothing to the child, but she senses the difference. Unable to verbalize her emotions, the young girl continues to do the usual things like play with her dolls and draw with crayons, but she also decides not to speak. It is as if she believes that speaking – words themselves – might be the actual cause of all their problems. *Alexandra's Project* (2003) also deals with the breakdown of a family. Released in 2003, the film divided audiences and critics: 'some credited it with saving their marriage, others accused it of ruining theirs' ('Production Notes', Vertigo Productions website). The traumatic breakdown of a relationship that involves children is also at the heart of this film. Steve is a middle-management office worker with a wife called Alexandra and two children. Having just received a promotion, he returns home on the evening of his birthday expecting some kind of happy family celebration only to discover the house is empty. All he finds is a videotape with a note saying, 'Surprise! Watch me.' And he does. Initially, his wife and children appear, sending him birthday greetings but then his children leave and, much to Steve's delight, his wife begins an erotic striptease. Things begin to sour when their male neighbour appears on the tape and the striptease evolves into a scene of adultery. The action then turns nasty, with Steve realising he is a prisoner in the house, with the locks changed, the security shutters closed and the battery of his mobile phone replaced by a single bullet. While the action is centred on the adults, the children haunt the film as shadowy witnesses to their parents' crumbling relationship, and their own shattered home.

The director's fascination with familial relationships and preoccupation with childhood are also focal points of *Bad Boy Bubby*:

> In some way I wanted to make a film about childhood. But, ultimately, I ended up with a decision to explore this through the dark side, if you like; I wanted to deal with certain aspects of child abuse and associated issues. I was thinking that if I really wanted to deal with it in a confronting way in a really low-budget film, then it might be better to do it somehow with an adult rather than an actual child. I was concerned about the process of doing the film with a child; I hadn't worked out what would happen to that child. I had worries about involving children in that sort of confrontational material. So that's the way it came about. (quoted in Malone, 2001b, p. 59)

In a television interview in 2011 with the theologian Scott Stephens, de Heer further discussed his ideas about childhood and the impact *Bad Boy Bubby* had had on audiences. Stephens hosts a programme on the Australian public-broadcast channel ABC1 entitled 'Life's Big Questions'. Interviewees are drawn from the whole gamut of Australian society, including politics, religion, medicine, science and the arts. The uniting factor that defines the theme of the show is that each individual usually has a religious belief or is guided by a moral compass that directly affects their actions, behaviour and work. Stephens's questions are broad but they nearly always devolve down to the impact of spirituality and religious beliefs on an individual's life. De Heer was an interesting choice as his public platforms generally involve publicity for his own films, Australian cinema in general and particularly low-budget production. Yet there is a kind of zeal to many of the director's beliefs about the current state of the world in which we live, particularly in relation to childhood. In more recent years, de Heer has also demonstrated a desire to explore Australia's brutal colonial history and the current state of indigenous rights and welfare. Agreeing with Stephens that he is a kind of missionary who just can't help himself, de Heer comments, 'there is an idealism that comes from innocence that is worth more than anything in terms of the human spirit' (2011).

Stephens suggests that this prolific director, with his oddball oeuvre, is in fact the most 'Christian' of film-makers, with *Bad Boy Bubby* winning an OCIS Award and *Dance Me to My Song* picking up the Australian Catholic Film Award in 1998 (Australian Catholic Film Office website). The director is not a religious man although he tries to be guided by a Christian principle: do unto others as you would have them do unto you. For him, innocence is 'worth more than anything in terms of the human spirit' and he finds it tragic to see the innocence of childhood destroyed. Inevitably any discussion with the director comes back to the extraordinary effect *Bad Boy Bubby* continues to have on audiences. Asked to explain the film's impact, de Heer replied: 'There is something in that film, which speaks of redemption, and I think ultimately that's what tips people over' (Stephens, 2011).

# ✖ Part 6

LEGACY

At the Q & A session after the release of his 2012 feature film *The King Is Dead* at the Nova cinema in Melbourne, de Heer related a humorous anecdote about audiences and the cinema. The director described how as a young filmmaker his publicist had sent him a stack of forty-two reviews of his second feature film *Incident at Raven's Gate* after its release in the UK. The first reviewer began by stating: 'Australians make some very bad films and this is one of the worst.' Although shattered at this, de Heer continued to read. The reviews were arranged from worst to best and, by the time he arrived at the final one, he was being likened to Tarkovsky in the singularity of his vision. The experience shaped his future understanding of the cinema and its audience. De Heer finds it best not to lead an audience by telling them what a film is about, and he is still surprised to discover how unique viewers' experiences can be. Yet some cinematic moments are able to prompt a more universal response. Audiences, critics and scholars alike have struggled with the cat scenes in *Bad Boy Bubby*, finding them callous, offensive and cruel. Yet this is an award-winning film with a unique vision; one that also deserves to be remembered for its commemoration of the durability of the human spirit. We recognise in Bubby's traumatic but redemptive story the power of social inclusion, whereby friendship, kindness and love can effect a kind of cure. Yet this is a film that might have had a very different ending.

One night driving home after finishing work on the shoot for the day, de Heer was stunned to hear a discussion on the radio about the possible reintroduction of the death penalty in Australia. He was so angered by this idea that he decided, then and there, to change the film's ending. Instead of a scene of domestic bliss, the denouement of the film would involve Bubby's arrest. The final moments would show him being hanged for his crimes. Once his anger had subsided, de Heer soon realised that this would not be a logical conclusion. Bubby might be 'guilty', but with his limited knowledge base,

Figure 14: The conclusion of the film is a joyous scene of domestic bliss.

'guilty of what?' (2010b). The director decided to return to the original ending – an overhead tracking shot takes us up over an industrial landscape and down to reveal Bubby in a kind of green oasis (see Figure 14). The final shots are uplifting, finding Bubby in a garden playing with his children, while their mother sits stroking a new pet kitten.

It is difficult to assess the legacy of *Bad Boy Bubby*; it is a film that still polarizes audiences. Time has not mellowed the impact of its confrontational and, at times, bizarre content. Needless to say, the film radically changed Nicholas Hope's career trajectory as an actor. As I have previously noted, while he was feted on the festival circuit, he spent many years on unemployment benefits struggling to find work. His autobiography, *Brushing the Tip of Fame*, traces the aftermath of this career-defining performance as Bubby and how the film has affected his life. His career has never revisited the heady heights he experienced at the Venice Film Festival and the AFI Awards, but the film's notoriety resulted in film-makers such as the independent American director Hal Hartley inviting him to screentest for one of his films. Hartley chose him for the part of Father Hawkes in his 1997 production *Henry Fool*. Hope also starred in the Australian director Paul Cox's satire *Lust and Revenge* (1996) and has taken various small roles in popular American films such as *Scooby-Doo* (2002) and *Anaconda – The Hunt for the Blood Orchid* (2004). Now spending his time between Australia, Norway and the UK, he has also worked in theatre and as an acting coach. In discussing *Bad Boy Bubby*, Hope is adamant that he will never work with animals again; that the film launched his career as a known actor on the international scene; but that it also resulted in him being typecast as a 'weird one' – an actor to whom you send all of those oddball roles (2004).

While de Heer has continued to write, produce and direct a range of generally low-budget features, it is *Bad Boy Bubby*, his first writing/directing project that launched his career on the international film-making circuit. He still predominantly works on low-budget productions, his most successful recent film being the indigenous-language production *Ten Canoes*, which won Un Certain Regard, the Special Jury Prize at Cannes and the Australian Film Institute Best Film Award in 2006. Now considered an 'elder' of the Australian cinema, he is also called upon as a public commentator, whose views on the film industry, religion and indigenous affairs are frequently quoted in the media. Cat controversy aside, de Heer has noted that he is 'surprised still by the phenomenon [*Bad Boy Bubby*] has become' (2010b):

> [T]he response to *Bad Boy Bubby* was quite unexpected yet extraordinary. There is something in that film, which speaks of redemption, and I think ultimately that's what tips people over. ... one of the things I wanted to do with that film is to say with enough love, care and attention, that the cycle that happens from abused child who grows up and becomes an abusive parent ... this cycle can be broken with more love, more care, more attention ... it's worth going on, it's possible, happiness is possible. (Stephens, 2011)

*Bad Boy Bubby* takes us on an extraordinary journey from the suffocating *huit clos* of the first act with Bubby essentially unsocialized, through a myriad of social exchanges which ultimately complete him, leaving him at the end fully formed as a friend, lover, father and charismatic performer. The film's significance lies in its depiction of a kind of social salvation, with its humanity and its experimental nature ensuring its longevity and its controversial but 'classic' status.

# APPENDICES

# Appendix A: Key Details

## Cast

| | | | |
|---|---|---|---|
| Bubby | Nicholas Hope | Vicki | Nellie Egan |
| Mom | Claire Benito | The Animal | Michael Constantinou |
| Pop | Ralph Cotterill | Prison Superintendent | Alec Talbot |
| Yobbo | Syd Brisbane | The Scientist | Norman Kaye |
| Screaming Woman | Nikki Price | Fondled Woman | Michelle O'Regan |
| Robbed Woman | Ullie Birve | Penniless Drunk | Gordon Poole |
| Fondled Salvo | Audine Leith | Number One Fan | Jamie Nicolai |
| Cherie the Salvo | Natalie Carr | Pandy | Pandy Tsimboulis |
| Pizza Waitress | Lucia Mastrantone | Rachael | Rachael Huddy |
| Angel | Carmel Johnson | Maryla | Maryla Galus |
| Treelopper | Jip de Heer | Janet | Janet Kanda |
| Little | James Ammitzboll | Heather | Heather Slattery |
| Salesman | Grant Piro | Shannon | Fille Dussellee |
| Woman in Mercedes | Celine O'Leary | Sharon | Stephanie Cooper |
| Cop/Warder | Dave Flannagan | Angel's Mother | Bridget Waters |
| Paul (band singer) | Paul Philpot | Angel's Father | Graham Duckett |
| Little Greg (keyboards) | Todd Telford | | |
| Big Greg (drummer) | Paul Simpson | *Others* | |
| Middle Greg (bass) | Stephen Smooker | Andy McPhee | Tim Maloney |
| Steve (guitarist) | Peter Monaghan | Geoff Revell | Lindsay Grose |
| Mark (roadie) | Mark Brouggy | Susan Ferguson | Josie Scattergood |
| Young Man | James Bonifazio | Alan Huddleston | Laurel Aird |
| Violinist | Emma West | Paul Ammitzboll | Fran O'Donoghue |
| Dan | Bruce Gilbert | Vincenzo Andreacchio | Clement de Salamanca |
| Cop #2 | Michael Habib | Olly Alick | Ryder Grindle |
| Cop #3 | Alan Holy | Kris Stewart | Jon Rossiter |
| Gayle | Betty Sumner-Lovett | | |

## Production Crew

| | | | |
|---|---|---|---|
| Director, Writer and Producer | Rolf de Heer | Art Direction | Tim Nicholls |
| Producer | Giorgio Draskovic | Production Management | Paul Ammitzboll, Sharon Jackson and Gina Ploenges |
| Associate Producer | David Lightfoot | | |
| Producer | Domenico Procacci | Assistant Director | Paul Ammitzboll |
| Supervising DOP | Ian Jones | Art Department | Crispin Joos |
| Sound Designer | James Currie | Binaural Sound Engineers | Frederick and Margaret Stahl |
| Film Editing | Suresh Ayyar | | |
| Production Design | Mark Abbott | Visual Effects | Molle DeBartolo |
| Costume Design | Beverly Freeman | Still Photographer | Simon Cardwell |
| Composer | Graham Tardiff | Work Experience | Tom Heuzenroeder |
| Casting | Audine Leith | | |

## Contributing Cinematographers in Order of Appearance

| | | | |
|---|---|---|---|
| Ian Jones | Gerald Thompson | John Armstrong | Geoffrey Simpson |
| Paul Dalwitz | Richard Michalak | Ernie Clarke | Steve McDonald |
| Kim Vaitiekus | John Chataway | Brian Bosisto | Roger Lanser |
| Rick Martin | Jeff Morgan | Brigid Costello | Simon Cardwell |
| Clive Duncan | John Ogden | Brendan Lavelle | Richard Rees-Jones |
| Ross Blake | Barry Helleren | Lisa Tomasetti | David Foreman |
| Steve Arnold | Tibor Hegedis | Harry Glynatsis | Max Pepper |
| David Burr | Paul Ammitzboll | Walter Holt | |

## Technical Specs

Runtime: 114 minutes
Sound Mix: Dolby
Colour: Colour
Aspect Ratio: 2.35.1
Technovision Camera and Lenses
DFL – Digital Film Laboratory, Australia
Film Length: 3118 meters

Print Film Format: 35 mm (Kodak)
Aspect Ratio: 2.35 : 1

## *Other Details*

### *Film Locations*
Adelaide, North Adelaide, Port Adelaide, South Adelaide, Semaphore, Thebarton, South Australia, Australia

### *Filming Dates*
16 November 1992–30 January 1993

### *Production Companies*
Bubby Productions, Fandango (Rome), South Australian Film Commission

### *Classification and Certification*
Argentina: 18
Australia: R
Canada: 16+
Finland: K-16
France: -12
Iceland: 16
New Zealand: R18
Sweden: 15
United Kingdom: 18 (re-released uncut, 2007)

## Appendix B: Notes

**1** A point of clarity about Bubby's age: 'He's been in his room for 35 years. It's time to let him out.' This is the byline on the website for Vertigo Productions (http://www.vertigoproductions.com.au/), the company founded in 1996 by the Italian producer Domenico Procacci along with Bryce Menzies and de Heer, as a vehicle for de Heer's films. The synopsis then goes on to talk about Bubby as thirty-eight years of age, but most other information, including the press kit and press releases, describe him as thirty-five.
**2** See for example Pearce (1994), pp. 14–15; Stephens (2011); Caputo and Burton (2002, pp. 47–55); de Heer and Overton, 'In Conversation', Australian Film Commission Archive; Malone (2001b), pp. 57–71; Cherchi Usai (2007).
**3** In 1992, the High Court of Australia's Mabo decision, which recognized native title, effectively overturned the doctrine of terra nullius. In *Australian Cinema after Mabo* (2004) Felicity Collins and Therese Davis examine how the High Court decision abruptly ended the colonial myth of white settlers' discovery of Australia as an empty land, and the ways in which this decision has been explored and wrestled with in post-1992 Australian cinema.
**4** De Heer claims not to have seen either of these films before making *Bad Boy Bubby* (see Pearce (1994), p. 14).
**5** The following quotations regarding cuts made to a range of films are taken from the BBFC files. The references are listed in the Works Cited under BBFC and each film's title.

## Appendix C: References

American Humane Association website, Findings on Films, 'Movie Review – Heaven's Gate', available from http://www.americanhumanefilmtv.org/movie-review-archives/ (accessed 24 March 2012).

Andrews, Nigel (1994) 'Arts – Problem Mothers – Cinema', *Financial Times*, 29 September, available from FACTIVA (accessed 25 October 2012).

Animal Rights Community website, 'Movies to Avoid: (Cruelty/ Killing)', forum posted 31 October 2012, available from http://www.animalsuffering.com/forum/viewtopic.php?t=3609&start=30 (accessed 1 July 2012).

'Animal Welfare Act 2006', *British Board of Film Classification Guidelines (*2009), available from http://www.legislation.gov.uk/ukpga/2006/45/contents (accessed 25 March 2012).

Anonymous (2011) 'Film about Anti-gay Preacher Who Murders Homosexuals Sparks Protests at Sundance Festival', *Daily Mail*, 24 January, available from http://www.dailymail.co.uk/news/article-1350065/Sundance-2010-Preacher-murders-homosexuals-film-sparks-protests.html (accessed 20 February 2011).

Anonymous (2010) '"Comment", Banned: Most Controversial Films Ever', *Belfast Telegraph*, 12 October, available from Proquest Central (accessed 1 November 2012).

Anonymous (2008) 'Hound Dog Director Says Dakota Fanning Rape Scene Was All Technical', *Starpulse.com*, 30 September, available from: http://www.starpulse.com/news/index.php/2008/09/30/hounddog_director_says_dakota_fanning_ra (accessed 20 February 2011).

Anonymous (2000) 'Filmmakers Accused of Animal Cruelty', *Vancouver Sun*, 28 August, p. A. 2.

Anonymous (1997) 'Film Blamed in Murder', *Bendigo Advertiser*, 23 May, p. 5.

Anonymous (1997) 'Maximum Jail for "Bad Boy"', *Herald Sun*, 7 June, p. 13.

Anonymous (1994) 'Bad Boy Runs into Flak', *Sydney Morning Herald*, 21 November, p. 17.

Anonymous (1993) 'Venice Film Festival: Childish', *Economist* vol. 328 no. 7829, p. 96.

Australian Catholic Film Office website (ACFO), http://www.catholic.org.au/index.php?option=com_content&view=article&id=1870:richard-leonard&catid=100:film-reviews-2010&Itemid=376 (accessed 2 July 2012).

Australian Government Classification website, 'Film Festivals and Community Screenings', available from http://www.classification.gov.au/www/cob/classification.nsf (accessed 9 April 2011).

Australian Government Classification website, 'Guidelines for the Classification of Films and Computer Games', available from http://www.comlaw.gov.au/Details/F2008C00126 (accessed 14 February 2012).

Australian Government Classification website, 'The 2007 Film Festival Guidelines', available from: http://www.classification.gov.au/Industry/Journal/Pages/Resources/Film%20Festival%20Guidelines%202007.pdf (accessed 9 April 2011).

Australian Government Classification website, '2003–2004 Annual Report of the Classification Boards', available from www.classification.gov.au (accessed 20 November 2011).

Australian Government, Department of the Environment, Water, Heritage and the Arts (2008) 'Threat Abatement Plan for Predation of Feral Cats', available from http://www.environment.gov.au/biodiversity/threatened/publications/tap/cats08.html (accessed 19 June 2012).

Australian Government, Department of Sustainability, Environment, Water, Population and Communities (2001) 'The Feral Cat (*Felis Catus*)', available from http://www.environment.gov.au/biodiversity/invasive/publications/pubs/cat.pdf (accessed 19 June 2012).

Australian Government, 'State and Territory Government', available from http://australia.gov.au/about-australia/our-government/state-and-territory-government (accessed 15 February 2012).

Badham, Katie (1993) '*Bad Boy Bubby* 1993', available from http://www.imdb.com/reviews/99/9934.html (accessed 5 February 2012).

Barber, Lynden (1997) 'Animal Act Adds Bite to Film Welfare,' *Australian*, 4 October, p. 10.

Barber, Lynden (1995) *Weekend Australian*, 11 February, p. 13.

**bad boy bubby** 115

BBFC website, '*Hannibal Holocaust*', available from http://www.bbfc.co.uk/BVV102579 (accessed 24 March 2011).

BBFC website, 'How to Get a Theatrical Work Classified', available from http://bbfc.co.uk/customers/theatrical/how-to-get-a-theatrical-work-classified (accessed 9 April 2011).

BBFC website, '*The Isle*', available from http://www.bbfc.co.uk/AFF169935 (accessed 24 March 2011).

BBFC website, '*The Legend of the Lone Ranger*', available from http://www.bbfc.co.uk/BVF041925 (accessed 24 March 2011).

BBFC website, 'The Licensing Act 2003', available from http://www.bbfc.co.uk/classification/guidelines/legal-considerations/ (accessed 1 November 2012).

BBFC website, '*Rambo III*', available from http://www.bbfc.co.uk/BVF061464 (accessed 24 March 2011).

BBFC website, '*Reds*', available from http://www.bbfc.co.uk/BVF021185 (accessed 24 March 2011).

Beilby, P. and Lansell, R. (eds) (1983) *Australian Motion Picture Yearbook 1983*, Melbourne: 4 Seasons.

Birnie, Peter (1994) 'Beauty and the Bleak Abound as Movie Mania Grips Town', *Vancouver Sun*, 29 September, available from FACTIVA (accessed 12 October 2012).

Brand, Jeffrey E. (2001) 'A Review of the Classification Guidelines for Films and Computer Games, Assessment of Public Submission on the Discussion Paper and Draft Revised Guidelines', Office of Film and Literature Classification, 11 February.

Breznican, Anthony (2007) 'Fanning Speaks up on Rape Scene', *USA Today*, 23 January, available from http://www.usatoday.com/life/movies/news/2007-01-23-fanning-hounddog_x.htm (accessed 20 February 2012).

Brook, Stephen (1997) 'Life for Bad Boy Bubby, Cling Wrap Killing of Girl', *Weekend Australian*, 7 June, p. 11.

Brown, Les (1988) *Cruelty to Animals: The Moral Debt*, Basingstoke: Macmillan.

Byrnes, Paul (1993) '*Bad Boy Bubby* 1993, Curator's Notes', Australian Screen website, available from http://aso.gov.au/titles/features/bad-boy-bubby/notes/ (accessed 9 April 2011).

BVA British Veterinary Association website, http://www.bva.co.uk/atoz/Tail_docking_of_dogs.aspx (accessed 7 March 2012).

Caputo, R. and Burton, G. (eds) (2002) *Third Take: Australian Film-makers Talk*, Crows Nest: Allen & Unwin.

Cardy, Tom (2007) 'Fast-tracked to Comedy Stardom', *Dominion Post*, 18 May, p. B9.

Cartwright, Lisa (1995) *Screening the Body: Tracing Medicine's Visual Culture*, Minneapolis: University of Minnesota Press.

CBD Council of Docked Breed website, http://www.cdb.org/ (accessed 7 March 2012).

Cerebral Palsy Alliance website, http://www.cerebralpalsy.org.au/about-cerebral-palsy/basic-guide-to-cerebral-palsy (accessed 1 July 2012).

Cherchi Usai, P. (2007) 'De Heer, Rolf: Oral History. Part Two', National Sound and Film Archive, Canberra, A.C.T.

'Cinematograph Films (Animals) Act 1937', Legislation.gov.uk website, available from http://www.legislation.gov.uk/ukpga/Edw8and1Geo6/1/59/contents (accessed 10 April 2012).

CIWF Compassion in World Farming website (2010) 'Australia Exporting Live Sheep to an often Cruel Death', 19 November, available from http://www.ciwf.org.uk/news/transport_of_live_animals/australia_exporting_live_sheep_to_an_often_cruel_death.aspx (accessed 24 March 2012).

Clark, Emily (2011) 'Counter-protests Await Westboro Church at Sundance', ABC 4.com, 24 January, available from http://www.abc4.com/content/news/state/story/Counter-protests-await-Westboro-Church-at-Sundance/DNKFNEmslEy5Rzgx727Y0A.cspx (accessed 20 February 2012).

Collins, Felicity and Davis, Therese (2004) *Australian Cinema after Mabo*, Cambridge: Cambridge University Press.

Craig, Benjamin (2004) *Sundance: A Festival Virgin's Guide: Surviving Park City and Thriving at America's Most Important Film Festival*, London: Cinemaimages Media.

Daly, Winkler (1994) 'An Innocent Thrown into an Ugly World', *Canberra Times*, 12 August, p. 12.

de Heer, Rolf (2010a) 'Audio Commentary' with Nicholas Hope, *Bad Boy Bubby*, Blu-ray Disc, Umbrella Entertainment. Released 13 October (Australia). Originally appeared on the 2 Disc (Collector's Edition) released by Umbrella 15 July 2005.

de Heer, Rolf (2010b) 'Christ Kid: You're a Weirdo', and *Bad Boy Bubby*, Blu-ray Disc, Umbrella Entertainment. Released 13 October (Australia). Originally appeared on the 2 Disc (Collector's Edition) released by Umbrella 15 July 2005.

de Heer, Rolf (2008) 'the dreaming … or not?', in Peter Cochrane (ed.) *Great Australians*, Sydney: William Heinemann, pp. 115–17.

de Heer, Rolf (1996) *Bad Boy Bubby*, Sydney: Currency Press.

de Heer, Rolf and Overton, Julia, 'In Conversation', Australian Film Commission Archive, available from http://afcarchive.screenaustralia.gov.au/newsandevents/afcnews/converse/rolf_deheer/newspage_135.aspx (accessed 16 May 2011).

de Valck, Marijke (2007) *Film Festivals: From European Geopolitics to Global Cinephilia*, Amsterdam: Amsterdam University Press.

Dermody, Susan and Jacka, Elizabeth (1987) *The Screening of Australia: Anatomy of a Film Industry*, vol. 1, Sydney: Currency Press.

Ellis, Katie (2011) 'Social Responsibility: Disability in Rolf de Heer's Early Films', *Metro Magazine* no. 169, pp. 106–10.

Ellis, Katie (2008) *Disabling Diversity: The Social Construction of Disability in 1990s Australian National Cinema*, Saarbruken: VDM Verlag Dr. Muller.

Ferman, James (1998) 'Cruelty in Films', *The Times*, 2 June, p. 21.

Film Victoria, 'Australian Films at the Australian Box Office', available from http://film.vic.gov.au/resources/documents/AA4_Aust_Box_office_report.pdf (accessed 16 May 2011).

Finlan, James (2005) 'Oedipus Down Under', *The Film Writings of James Finlan*, blog, available from http://eireville.blogspot.com.2005/10/bad-boy-bubby.html (accessed 20 July 2010).

Fish, Stanley (2010) 'The First Amendment and Kittens', *New York Times*, 26 April, available from http://opinionator.blogs.nytimes.com/2010/04/26/the-first-amendment-and-kittens/ (accessed 20 March 2011).

Fitzgerald, Michael (1994) 'Hanging Loose', *Who Weekly*, 29 August, pp. 38–40.

George, Sandy (1994) 'De Heer Praises Talented Team on Low-budget "Bubby"', *Encore*, 14–27 November, p. 6.

Gibbons, Fiachra (2001) 'Dogfight Looms on Showing Feted Films', *Guardian*, 20 February, p. 5.

Govtrack.us website, 'Bill H.R. 5566', available from www.govtrack.us (accessed 15 November 2012).

Green, J. L. (2011) Chief Assistant (policy) BBFC, email to the author, 18 April.

'Guidelines for the Safe Use of Animals in Filmed Media', American Humane Association, available from http://www.americanhumane.org/assets/pdfs/animals/pa-film-guidelines.pdf (accessed 24 March 2011).

Hawker, Phillipa (1995) 'Incident at Raven's Gate', in Scott Murray (ed.) *Australian Film 1978–1994: A Survey of Theatrical Features*, Melbourne: Oxford University Press, Australian Film Commission and Cinema Papers.

Hicky-Moody, Anna and Iocco, Melissa (2004) 'Sonic Affect (s): Binaural Technologies and the Construction of Auratorship in Rolf de Heer's *Bad Boy Bubby*', *Metro Magazine* no. 140, pp. 78–81.

Hope, Cat (2004) 'Hearing the Story: Sound Design in the Films of Rolf de Heer', *Senses of Cinema* no. 31, available from http://www.sensesofcinema.com/2004/31/sound_design_rolf_de_heer/ (accessed 8 April 2011).

Hope, Nicholas (2004) *Brushing the Tip of Fame*, Sydney: Bantam.

Hope, Nicholas (2010) 'Popcorn Taxi Q & A', *Bad Boy Bubby*, Blu-ray Disc, Umbrella Entertainment. Released 13 October (Australia). Originally appeared on the 2 Disc (Collector's Edition) released by Umbrella on 15 July 2005.

Hoyle, Ben (2006) 'Festival Pulls Film That Violates Animal Cruelty Law', *Ottawa Citizen*, 24 August, p. E.5.

H.R. 5566 (111th): Animal Crush Video Prohibition Act of 2010, Govtrack.us website, available from http://www.govtrack.us/congress/bills/111/hr5566 (accessed 12 April 2012).

Humane Society of the United States Organisation website, 'About Us: Overview: The Humane Society of the United States', http://www.humanesociety.org/about/overview/ (accessed 11 April 2012).

Jameson, Julietta (1994) 'The Black in Bubby', *Telegraph-Mirror*, 9 July, pp. 100–1.

Johnston, Sheila (1994) 'FILM', *Independent*, 30 September, available from Proquest Central (accessed 9 October 2012).

Johnstone, Iain (1994) 'Queens of the Road; Cinema', *The Times*, 16 October, available from Proquest Central (accessed 12 October 2012).

Kalof, Linda and Fitzgerald, Amy (eds) (2007) *The Animals Reader: The Essential Classic and Contemporary Writings*, Oxford and New York: Berg.

Kennedy, Harlan (1993) 'Festivals: Venice, Monstra Happy Fella', *Film Comment* no. 29 (November), pp. 64–6.

Kermode, Mark (2012) 'AND THE WINNER IS: Movie critic Mark Kermode reveals his favourite big-screen moments of all time', *Freelibrary*, available from http://www.thefreelibrary.com/..AND+THE+WINNER+IS%3b+Movie+critic+Mark+Kermode+reveals+his+favourite+...-a0201726667 (accessed 12 October 2012).

Lee, Charles Jason (2005) 'Shamans, Sex Beasts and Abuse: Mother–Son Relationships in Popular and Cult Cinema', *Film International* no. 15, pp. 22–31.

Legislation.gov.uk website, 'The Animal Welfare Act 2006', available from http://www.legislation.gov.uk/ukpga/2006/45/contents (accessed 10 April 2012).

Lippit, Akira Mizuta (2002) 'The Death of an Animal', *Film Quarterly* vol. 56 no. 1 (Fall), available from http://ucpressjournals.com/journal.php?j=fq (accessed 21 March 2012).

Liptak, Adam (2010) 'Justices Reject Ban on Videos of Animal Cruelty', *New York Times*, 20 April, available from http://www.nytimes.com/2010/04/21/us/21scotus.html?_r=1&pagewanted=print (accessed 20 March 2011).

Lowing, Rob (1994) 'The Ugly Australian in Focus', *Sun Herald*, 31 July, available from FACTIVA (accessed 9 October 2012).

Lucas, Rose (1998) 'Dragging It Out: Tales of Masculinity in Australian Cinema, from *Crocodile Dundee* to *Priscilla, Queen of the Desert*', *Journal of Australian Studies* vol. 22 no. 56, pp. 138–46.

Lyttle, John (1993) 'FILM', *Independent*, 8 October, available from Proquest Central (accessed 12 October 2012).

Macdonald, J. M. (1963) 'The Threat to Kill', *American Journal of Psychiatry* vol. 120, pp. 125–30.

Malcolm, Derek (1993) 'Undisputed Campion: Her First Cannes Feature Screening Ended in Tears, but Jane Campion Has Since Captured the Critic's Hearts and the Coveted Palme D'Or with *The Piano*', *Guardian*, 22 October.

Malone, Peter (2008) 'From Conflict to Reconciliation in World Cinema', *Studies in World Christianity* vol. 14 no. 2, pp. 108–24.

Malone, Peter (2002) 'Social Communications to Media', *Compass: A Review of Topical Theology* vol. 36 no. 3 (Spring), available from http://compassreview.org/Spring02/4html (accessed 5 February 2012).

Malone, Peter (2001a) 'Les Jurys d' Église dans les Festivals de cinéma', available from http://www.officecom.qc.ca/indexSiteOCS/Jury/malonefr.html (accessed 5 February 2012).

Malone, Peter (2001b) *Myth and Meaning: Australian Film Directors in Their Own Words*, Sydney: Currency Press.

Martin, Adrian (2010) 'Ozploitation Compared to What? A Challenge to Contemporary Australian Film Studies', *Studies in Australasian Cinema* vol. 4 no. 1, pp. 9–21.

Martin, Douglas (1999) 'Caution: Exploding Donkey', *New York Times*, 9 May, p. 4.

McKee, Alan, Albury, Katherine and Lumby, Catharine (2008) *The Porn Report*, Melbourne: University of Melbourne.

Merz-Perez, Linda and Heide, Kathleen M. (2004) *Animal Cruelty: Pathway to Violence against People*, Oxford: Altimira Press.

Metherell, Lexi (2009) 'More Controversy on the Melbourne International Film Festival', ABC, 27 July, available from http://www.abc.net.au/worldtoday/content/2009/s2637439.htm (accessed 5 February 2012).

Min, Lim Li (1997) 'De Heer out on a Cinematic Limb', *New Straits Times*, 26 April, p. 3.

Morris, Rick (1993) 'South Australian Film Scoops Top Film Awards', Press Release from Minister of Arts and Cultural Heritage, 13 September.

O'Grady, Desmond (1994) 'Bad Boy Bubby's Cat Gets Attention from Italian Law', *Age*, 8 December, p. 20.

Orange, Michelle (2008) 'Hounddog', *Village Voice*, 17 September, available from http://www.villagevoice.com/2008-09-17/film/hounddog/ (accessed 27 February 2011).

O'Regan, Tom (1996) *Australian National Cinema*, London and New York: Routledge.

Parliament of Australia website, Commonwealth of Australia Constitution Act Chapter I. The Parliament. Part V – Powers of the Parliament, Section 51, available from http://www.aph.gov.au/About_Parliament/Senate/Powers_practice_n_procedures/Constitution/par5cha1 (accessed on 15 February 2012).

Pearce, David (1994) 'Rolf de Heer on Bubby', *Movie Trader*, August, pp. 14–15.

Pullar, Ellen (2006) 'Jane Campion: Biography', *Jane Campion: Cinema, Nation, Identity*, Dunedin: University of Otago Press, available from http://www.otago.ac.nz/communicationstudies/campion/biography.html (accessed 19 January 2012).

Rayner, Jonathan (2000) *The Contemporary Australian Cinema*, Manchester: Manchester University Press.

Robinson, David (1993) 'Carving a Novel out of Short Stories; Venice Film Festival; Cinema', *The Times*, 13 September, available from http://www.thetimes.co.uk (accessed 4 April 2011).

Rosen, Alan, Walter, Garry, Politis, Tom and Shortland, Michael (1997) 'From Shunned to Shining: Doctors, Madness and Psychiatry in Australian and New Zealand Cinema', *MJA* no. 167, pp. 640–4.

Rouyer, Philippe and Ciment, Michel (1995) 'Rolf de Heer', *Positif* no. 417, pp. 4–13.

RSPCA website, 'Our History-About Us-RSPCA in Action', available from http://www.rspca.org.uk/in-action/aboutus/heritage (accessed 10 April 2012).

Russell, Mark (1997) 'Wrapped up in Violence', *Herald Sun*, 31 May, pp. 26–7.

SAG-AFTRA One Union website, 'Who Looks after the Well-being of Animals That Appear in Films and TV Shows?', http://www.sag.org/who-looks-after-well-being-animals-appear-films-and-tv-shows/ (accessed 24 March 2011).

SBBFC website, 'A Serbian Film – Srpski Film', http://www.sbbfc.co.uk/CaseStudies/A_Serbian_Film__Srpski_Film (accessed 9 April 2011).

Schembri, Jim (2008) 'DVD of the Week', *Age*, 31 May, available from http://www.theage.com.au (accessed 11 November 2010).

Screen Australia website, 'Productions: Bad Boy Bubby (1993)', available from http://www.screenaustralia.gov.au/find-a-film/detail.aspx?tid=6452 (accessed 7 March 2012).

SIGNIS: World Catholic Association for Communications website, http://www.signis.net/malone/tiki-index.php (accessed 5 February 2012).

Stahl, Frederick (2002) 'Standing Room Only for a Thunderbolt in a Wheelchair', *Sydney Morning Herald*, 31 October, available from http://www.smh.com.au/articles/2002/10/30/1035683471529.html (accessed 16 January 2012).

Starrs, D. Bruno (2010) 'The Aural Point of View in the Early Films of Rolf de Heer', *Quarterly Review of Film and Video* vol. 28 no. 1, pp. 28–40.

Starrs, D. Bruno (2009) *Dutch Tilt, Aussie Auteur: The Films of Rolf de Heer*, Saarbrücken: VDM Verlag, Dr Müller.

Starrs, D. Bruno (2008) '*Dance Me to My Song* (Rolf de Heer 1997): The Story of a Disabled Dancer', in Mark Harvey (ed.) *Proceedings Scopic Bodies Dance Studies Research Seminar Series*, Auckland: University of Auckland Press.

Starrs, D. Bruno (2006) 'The Audience as Aurator Again? Sound and Rolf de Heer's Ten Canoes', *Metro Magazine* no. 149, pp. 18–20.

State Government of Victoria, Department of Primary Industries website, 'Code of Practices for the Welfare of Film Animals', available from http://www.dpi.vic.gov.au/agriculture/about-agriculture/legislation-regulation/animal-welfare-legislation/codes-of-practice-animal-welfare/film-animals (accessed 12 March 2012).

Stephens, Scott (2011) 'Life's Big Questions: Rolf de Heer', *Compass* ABC1, 25 March, available from http://www.abc.net.au/compass/s3129922.htm (accessed 16 January 2012).

Stratton, David (1993) 'Bad Boy Bubby Review', *Variety*, 1 September, available from http://www.variety.com/review/VE1117901195 (accessed 30 March 2011).

Susskind, Anne (1994) 'Bring up Bubby', *HQ*, July–August, pp. 78–82.

Vertigo Productions, 'Press Kit 1985', Production Notes, Tail of a Tiger, available from http://www.vertigoproductions.com.au/information.php?film_id=9&display=notes (accessed 17 May 2011).

Vivarelli, Nick (2011) 'Procacci Courts Controversy in "Blood"', *Variety*, 14 May, available from http://www.variety.com/article/VR1118037050 (accessed 20 February 2012).

Vnuk, Helen (2003) 'Xrated? Outdated', *Age*, 20 September, available from http://www.theage.com.au/articles/2003/09/19/1063625202157.html (accessed 20 February 2012).

Waisman, Sonia S., Frasch, Pamela D. and Wagman, Bruce A. (2006) *Animal Law: Cases and Materials*, Durham, NC: Caroline Academic Press.

Wiseman, Andreas (2010) 'BBFC Cuts I Spit on Your Grave for Frightfest Screening; Festival Pulls a Serbian Film', *Screendaily*, 26 August, available from http://www.screendaily.com/festivals/other-festivals/bbfc-cuts-i-spit-on-your-grave-for-frightfest-screening-festival-pulls-a-serbian-film/5017458.article (accessed 22 March 2011).

Worthington, Anne (2011) 'Live Exports to Shamed Abattoirs Suspended', *Four Corners ABC News*, 1 June, available from http://www.abc.net.au/news/2011-05-31/live-exports-to-shamed-abattoirs-suspended/2738896 (accessed on 24 March 2012).

Zwar, Adam (1998) 'Outrage at Cruelty Film', *Sunday Herald Sun*, p. 19.

# Index

AFC (Australian Film Commission), 10
AFI (Australian Film Institute), 6
   Awards, 7, 21, 23, 27, 104–5
*Alexandra's Project* (2003), 98
Altman, Robert, 20
American Humane Association (AHA), 51, 52–5, 62, 113
Ammitzboll, Paul, 36
*Amores Perros* (2000), 52
*An Angel at My Table* (1990), 18, 95
*Anaconda – The Hunt for the Blood Orchid* (2004), 104
Andrews, Nigel, 86–7
Angel, xvii–xix, 12, 81, 85, 90–1, 94, 97
   Carmel Johnson, actor, xvii, 12, 82
animal cruelty, 36–41, 43–6
   and audience affect, 46–8
   and CGI, 55
   in fiction and non-fiction film, 46–7
   and human behaviour, aberrant, 47–8
   legal issue, xiii, 36, 40, 49–55
   and students' responses, 46–7
   treatment of horses in the cinema, 49–51
animal fights, 51
   cock fights, 51
   dog fights, 52, 55
   *see also Cockfighter* (1974)
Animal Liberation Victoria, 59, 82

animal-rights communities, x, xiv, 40
   and groups, 54, 59
   and campaigners, 61
Animal Rights Community website, 70
animal-rights laws, 36–8
   activism, 49, 55
   in Australia, 56–9, 61–2
   in the United Kingdom, 49–52
   in the United States, 49–55
Animal Welfare Act 2006, (UK), xii, 41, 49–51
Animal Welfare League of South Australia, 38, 40, 58, 81
Australia
   colonial history, 33–4, 100
   and the death penalty, 103
   and indigenous rights, 100
   and live cattle trade, 46–7
   masculinities, 90–1
   national cinema, xi, 5–6, 95–6
   'ozploitation', xii
   post-Mabo era, xi
   rating regulation discrepancies in the territories, 28–9
   state law variations, 57
   'ugly Australian', 87
Australian Classification Board, 61
Australian Department of the Environment, Water, Heritage and the Arts, 60

Australian Department of Primary
    Industries, 57
Australian Department of Sustainability,
    Environment, Water, Population and
    Communities, 60–1
Australian Government Classification
    website, 27–30, 37
Australian Screen website, 39
Ayyar, Suresh, 4

*Bad Boy Bubby* (1994)
    binaural sound recording, x, 13–14
    box office, Australia, 37
    budget, xiii, 6, 8, 10
    casting, xi, 11–12
    cinematographers, x, 10, 13
    distribution, xi, 21, 27, 31, 35–8, 62
    DVD and Blu-ray release, ix, 11, 16,
        31, 38–9, 51, 78, 81, 93
    media attention, x–xii, 20, 61–2, 65,
        85–90
    phenomenon, xi, 17, 23, 86, 105
band, alternative punk rock, xvi–xix, 85,
    94, 97
Barber, Lynden, xiii, 59
BBFC (British Board of Film
    Classification), 31, 37–8, 49–52, 77,
    112
*Being There* (1979), xii
Benito, Claire
    actress, theatre, 12
    and cat, 82
    as Mom, Florence (Flo), ix, xiii,
        xv–xvi, 12, 14, 16, 65–77, 90–2,
        94
Birnie, Peter, 86
blockbusters, Hollywood, 5, 7
bloggers, x, 40
Blue Underground, 36
breathing, 14, 74–82, 85
    suffocation, xii, xv–xvi, 36, 74–9, 80
    symbol, 82

Bubby, main character, ix, xii–xiii, xv–xix,
    12–18, 23, 36–7, 40, 65–82, 85–6,
    89–94, 96–7, 103–5
    and autism, 13
    cling-wrap killer, xvii–xviii
    communication, xv
    mimicry, xv–xviii, 68, 74–5, 85
    performance, xix, 11–12, 67, 85, 104
    as Pop, xviii, 85, 93–4
    *see under* Rolf de Heer
    *see also* Nicholas Hope
Byrnes, Paul, 39–40

Campion, Jane, 18
    *see under* film titles
Candide, ix, 19, 87
Cartwright, Lisa, 45
cats,
    and cruelty, x, xii–xiii, xvi, 17, 35–41,
        48, 55, 58–9, 67–70, 73–82, 88,
        103
    domestic, feral, stray, 40, 57, 59–62,
        69–70
    on set, xii–xiii, xv, xviii, 39, 58, 67–8,
        73
    prejudice, 59–61, 82
    TAP (Threat Abatement Plan), 60–1
censorship, x, xii–xiv, 27, 40–1, 49–55, 77
    in Australia, 56–62
    definition, 40–1
    in the UK, 49–52, 77
    in the US, 52–5
    *see under* crush videos; film festivals
Cerebral Palsy Alliance website, 93
Cinematograph Films (Animals) Act 1937
    (UK), 49–52
CARA (Classification and Rating
    Administration, US), 32
Clarke, Sue, 52
cling wrap, ix, xvi–xix, 36, 79–81, 88–9
*Cockfighter* (1974), 51
cockroaches, xv, xvii, 36, 68–70, 86

'Code of Practice for the Welfare of Film Animals' (Australia), 57–8
Collette, Toni, 95
CGI
    see under animal cruelty
*The Confessor Caresser* (1989), 11
Cotterill, Ralph, 11–12
    as Pop, xvi–xvii, 16, 90–1, 94
Cox, Paul, 104
criminal associations, 86–90
    copy-cat crimes, 88
    and Josef Fritzl, 90
    see also Keyte, Troy David
Cruelty to Animal Act of 1876 (UK), 49
crush videos, 55–6
    and Bill Clinton, 56
    and President Obama, 56
cult films, xi, xiii, 12, 36–7, 51, 91
Currie, James, 13, 17–18

*Dance Me to My Song* (1998), 14, 100
Davis, Miles, 7, 10
de Heer, Rolf
    and animal cruelty, x, 38–40, 58–9, 77, 81–2
    and *Bad Boy Bubby*, development and success, 17, 19, 36, 86, 92, 103
    biography, 3–11
    Bubby, casting, 11–12
    Bubby, character origins, 97
    career, 23–4, 105
    childhood, interest in, 97–100
    reputation, x, 21–2, 87, 103
    style, 13
    Vertigo Productions, 3–5, 93, 98, 112
    writer/director, 14, 105
    writing process, 8–10
    see under film titles
*De Profundis*
    see under OCIC
*Diaz – Don't Clean up This Blood* (2012), 10

*Dingo* (1991), 7–8, 10, 15, 96
disability, x, xii, 86, 92–7
    cerebral palsy, 93
    as a medical pathology, 95
    as a social model, 96
    as a theme, 86
Disability Rights movement, 96
Domarodzki, Jerzy, 95

Edinburgh Film Festival, 51
Edison, Thomas
    and the electrocution of animals, 45
*Electrocuting an Elephant* (1903), 45
    see also Topsy, the mankilling elephant
Ellis, Katie, 95–6
*The Enigma of Kaspar Hauser* (*Jeder für sich und Gott gegen alle*, 1974), xii
Entertainment Film Distribution, 37
*Epsilon* (1997), 96
Eureka Entertainment, 38
exploitation, film, xiii, 10

family relations
    father, ix, xii, xvi, 16, 80, 89, 90–2, 94–5. 105
    incest and fear, ix, xii, 20, 70–3, 92
    mother and son, 81, 86–8, 90–2
    Oedipal, 90–1
Fandango Company, 10
Fanning, Dakota, 33
feral children stories, xii
Ferman, James, 50–1
FFC (Film Finance Corporation, Australia), 6–7, 35
film classifications
    in Australia, 27–31, 37, 58–9, 61
    in the UK, 31–2, 37, 51, 77
    in the US, 32–5
film festivals, ix, x–xi, 4–7, 12, 14, 17–24, 27–36, 39, 51, 59, 62, 86–8, 98, 104
    and classification exemptions, 27–35
    see also festival titles

'Film Festivals and Community Screenings' (Australia), 28
Fish, Stanley, 56
Fitzgerald, Amy, 56–7
Flannaca, Bruno, 89
*Forrest Gump* (1994), xii
*Four Corners* (1961–), 46–7
   *see also* Indonesian abattoirs
Frame, Janet, 95
Freudian interpretation, 91–2
FrightFest, 31–2

Green, J. L., 37–8, 75, 77
Grenville, Kate, 95
'Guidelines for the Classification of Films and Computer Games' (Australia), 27, 58
'Guidelines for the Safe Use of Animals in Filmed Media' (US), 53
Gulpilil, David, 3–4
   *see also The Tracker* (2002)
*Gummo* (1997)
   and animal-rights protest, 59

Hartley, Hal, 104
Hauser, Kaspar, ix
*Heaven's Gate* (1980), 54
Heide, Kathleen, 48
Helfgott, David, 95
*Henry Fool* (1997), 104
*Henry: Portrait of a Serial Killer* (1993), 87
Herzog, Werner, ix, xii, 20
Hicks, Scott, 95
Hicky-Moody, Anna, x, 13
high concept, 5
Hope, Cat, x, 13–14
Hope, Nicholas
   and animal cruelty, 35–6, 39, 69, 77–8, 81–2, 105
   career, effect of starring in *Bad Boy Bubby*, 12, 19, 23, 104
   early life in South Australia, 11
   performance in *Bad Boy Buddy*, ix, 11–13, 86–7
   recollections, 17–18, 89
   *see under The Confessor Caresser* (1989)
*Hounddog* (2007)
   and controversy, 32–4
   *see also* Fanning, Dakota; Kampmeier, Deborah
humane societies
   *see under* titles
humanity, xi, 105

IMDb (International Movie Database), 70
Inarritu, Gonzales, 52
*Incident at Raven's Gate* (1987), 5–8, 11, 15, 103
Indonesian abattoirs, 46–7
innocence,
   and childhood, 7, 11, 97–100
   and exploitation, xiii, 33–4
   and redemption, 11
Iocco, Melissa, x, 13
Italian controversy,
   and boycott of Australian products, 38–40
   and President of Italy, Oscar Luigi Scalfaro, 39, 78
   and regional councillor, Michele Boato, 39, 79
   *see also* animal cruelty
Italian Society for the Prevention of Cruelty to Animals, 39

*Jaws* (1975), 5, 71
Jones, Alan, 31
Jones, Ian, 13
Johnston, Sheila, 86
Johnstone, Iain, 87

Kadeer, Rebiya, 30
Kalof, Linda, 47, 56

Kampmeier, Deborah, 32–4
*Ken Park* (2002), 29
Kennedy, Harlan, 19
   and the Sydney Film Festival, 29–30
Kermode, Mark, 88
Keyte, Troy David, 88–9
   *see also* criminal associations
Kieslowski, Krzysztof, 21
*The King Is Dead* (2012), x, 67, 103

*Ladybird, Ladybird* (1994), 20, 86
Lee, Charles Jason, 91
Legrand, Michel, 10
*Lilian's Story* (1996), 95
Linden, Rheya, 59, 82
Liptak, Adam, 55–6
   *see also* crush videos
Loach, Ken, 20, 86
Lockwood, Randall, 48
Lowenstein, Richard, 10
Lowing, Rob, 87
Lucas, Rose, 90–1
*Lust and Revenge* (1996), 104
Lyttle, John, 87

Macdonald, J. M., 47–8
   and the Macdonald Triad (triad of sociopathy), 47–8
Malone, Father Peter, 20–2, 98
   *see also* OCIC
Martin, Adrian, xii
Martin, Douglas, 55
mental illness, 89, 95
Merz-Perez, Linda, 48
Metherell, Lexi, 30–1
MIFF (Melbourne International Film Festival), 30–1
Min, Lim Li, 87
Mom,
   *see under* Benito, Claire
Moore, Richard, 30

moral compass, 100
MPAA (Motion Picture Association of America), 27

*Nanook of the North* (1922), 46
NATO (National Association of Theatre Owners, Inc., US), 32
Norway, 36, 104

OCIC (International Catholic Organization for Cinema), 17, 20–1
   *see also* Peter Malone, Father
Oedipal story, 91
OFLC (Office of Film and Literature Classification, Australia), 29–30
O'Grady, Desmond, 39
online communities, x, 34, 40
O'Regan, Tom, xiii, 5

Pearce, David, 9, 13–15, 112
*The Piano* (1993), 18
Pontecorvo, Gillo, 18
   *see under* Venice Film Festival
pressure groups, 32
   *see also* Westboro Baptist Church
Prevention of Cruelty to Animals Act (NSW 1979), 57
Procacci, Domenico, 10, 17, 39
   *see also* Diaz – *Don't Clean up This Blood* (2012)

*The Quiet Room* (1996), 98

Rachael, (Rachael Huddy), xviii, 81, 94, 96–7
*Red State* (2011), 32, 34–5
redemption, x, 11, 100, 105
   *see also* Smith, Kevin, 32, 34–5
religious sentiments, x, xiii, 20, 23, 27, 33, 95, 100
Robinson, David, 19

Rose, Heather (aka Heather Slattery), 14, 92–5
  and Frederick Stahl, 14, 92
  de Heer, working with, 93
  as Julie in *Dance Me to My Song* (1998), 14
RSPCA (Royal Society for the Prevention of Cruelty to Animals), xii, 47, 49–52, 57–9

SAG (Screen Actors Guild, US), 7, 53–4
Salvation Army, xiii, xvi, 14, 85, 87, 94, 97
Schweitzer, Albert, 52
*Scooby-Doo* (2002), 104
screenplay, *Bad Boy Bubby*, 9–10, 23, 97
  award, 23
  and Currency Press, 97
  *see also* de Heer, Rolf
*A Serbian Film* (2010), 31
sexual abuse,
  child exploitation, 33
  incest, ix, xii, 20, 70, 88, 90, 92–4
  sodomy, xviii, 85
  *see also* family relations
*Shine* (1996), 95
shoot, *Bad Boy Bubby*
  experimentation, x, 12, 49
  location, 12
*Short Cuts* (1993), 20
SIGNIS (World Catholic Association for Communication), 20–1
Singer, Ritchie, 11
Smith, Kevin, 32, 34–5
  *see also Red State*
*Snatch* (2000), 4, 51
social sentiments, xiv, 41
soundtrack, 10, 14, 67, 70, 79
South Australian State Government, 10
Stahl, Frederick, 13–14
  and ASIO (Australian Security Intelligence Organization), 13
  and Heather Rose, 92–3
  *see also* binaural sound recording
Starrs, D. Bruno, x, 3–4, 13–14
*Starship Troopers* (1997), 70
Stephens, Scott, x, 99–100, 105
Stratton, David, xiii
*Struck by Lightning* (1990), 95
Sundance Film Festival, 32–4
*Sweetie* (1989), 18, 95
Sydney Film Festival, 29–30

*Tail of a Tiger* (1984), 4, 98
TAP (Threat Abatement Plan)
  *see under* cats
'10BA Tax Concession for Film and Television Production', (Australia), 6
*Ten Canoes* (2006), x, 3–4, 105
*The Ten Conditions of Love* (2009), 30
  *see also* MIFF
*Three Colours Blue* (1993), 21–2
Topsy, the mankilling elephant, 45–6
  *see also Electrocuting an Elephant* (1903)
*The Tracker* (2002), x, 3–4,
'The 2007 Film Festival Guidelines', (Australia), 30

Umbrella, vii, 11, 16, 81, 96
UNDA (International Catholic Organization for Radio and Television), 20
United Kingdom,
  history of animal rights, xii, 49–52
  and Queen Victoria, 49
  Westminster Council and *A Serbian Film*, 31–2
United States
  and classification and rating rules, xii, 32, 52

Venice Film Festival (50th), x, xi, 17–19, 35–6, 39, 104
  *see also* film festivals; OCIC

Vertigo Productions
   *see under* de Heer, Rolf
Village Roadshow, 37

Waisman, Sonia, 53
*Wake in Fright* (1971), 61

Westboro Baptist Church
   hate organization, 34–5
   *see under Red State* (2011)
*The Wild Child* (*L'enfant sauvage,* 1970), xii
World Society for the Protection of
   Animals, 38, 54

www.ingramcontent.com/pod-product-compliance
Lightning Source LLC
Chambersburg PA
CBHW051813230426
43672CB00012B/2719